# Exploring Rural
# SCOTLAND

OTHER BOOKS IN THE *EXPLORING RURAL* SERIES

**Series Editor: Andrew Sanger**

*Austria*: Gretel Beer
*England & Wales*: Christopher Pick
*France*: Andrew Sanger
*Germany*: John Ardagh
*Greece*: Pamela Westland
*Ireland*: Andrew Sanger
*Italy*: Michael Leech
*Spain*: Jan S. McGirk

# Exploring Rural
# SCOTLAND

## GILBERT SUMMERS

**PASSPORT BOOKS**
a division of *NTC Publishing Group*
Lincolnwood, Illinois USA

# CONTENTS

# Contents

*To Beth*
*who has patience*

# ACKNOWLEDGEMENTS

I owe thanks to many of Scotland's area tourist board staff over the years who have given advice and assistance, especially James Fraser and David Wyles, Anne Burgess, Douglas Ritchie, Shirley Spain, Yvonne Cook, Jean Slessor, Scott Armstrong and Bruce Simpson. Special thanks for their hospitality are due to Andrew Llanwarne and Meta Maltman of Dumfries and Galloway Tourist Board, Charles Currie of Isle of Arran Tourist Board, and Libby Weir-Breen and Maurice Mullay of the Shetland Tourist Organisation. Sue Hall and John Hutchinson of the Scottish Tourist Board have also been helpful. Many other individuals working in the Scottish travel market have been kind and hospitable, including: Alasdair and Jane Robertson of the Holly Tree; John Rodger, Shetland Hotel; Iain Johnston and Brian Miller, Auchrannie House Hotel; Peter MacDougall, Corsemalzie House Hotel; Harry Steven; Scott Colegate, P&O Ferries; Murdo Grant (of the MV *Shearwater*); and especially Ian and Audrey Brown of Auchterarder House. Also numerous tourist information centre staff.

I owe special thanks to my mother and father, Catherine and Gilbert Summers, in Fraserburgh, who encouraged me to explore rural Scotland from an early age.

Most important of all, warmest love and thanks are owed to my wife Beth Ingpen: unofficial editor, mapping 'expert', relief driver, finder of missing pens and fiercest critic.

## Scotland—the regions and the routes

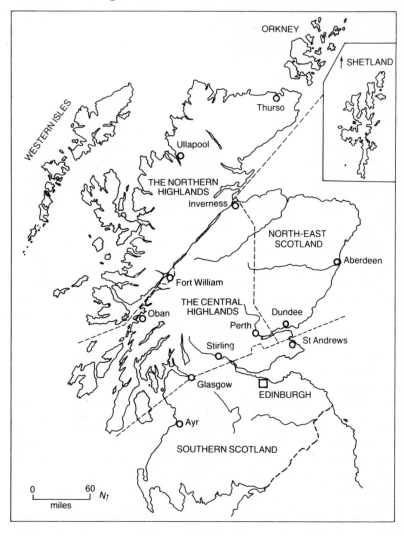

# INTRODUCTION

In 1707, after the final meeting of Scotland's own Parliament in the capital, Edinburgh, this once independent European nation became part of the United Kingdom. However, apart from sharing—broadly speaking—the same kind of language in most of the country, Scotland is different from other parts of the UK. Independent or not, Scots have stubbornly clung to their own identity, in spite of the levelling efforts, conscious or otherwise, of the media, government from London or waves of incomers from the south. They have also remained remarkably friendly.

Perhaps their still-surviving sense of identity is helped by the characteristics of the land which, particularly north and west of the Central Lowlands, is in many places rugged and uncompromising. These northern heartlands are also remote enough to generate excitement and a sense of adventure in even the least imaginative visitor.

In area, Scotland is about three-fifths the size of England. This book portrays the diversity of the 30,000sq. miles of Scotland, both Highland and Lowland, and looks at the regional differences to be found in its mostly thinly scattered population of 5.5 million. Though certain mapmakers' projections, which show the UK decreasing in size as it goes north, may mislead some first-time visitors, the text tries to give some sense of Scotland's relative size and scale. It prepares the visitor for the surprise of finding a signpost near Inverness announcing 'Wick 112 miles', yet reassures the traveller that it is perfectly possible to leave Edinburgh after breakfast, have morning coffee in Perth and reach Aviemore in time for lunch!

In fact, this book covers quite a few places where dawdling over coffee or lunch may be recommended. In Scotland, there is a wealth of interest waiting to be discovered—which makes journey times quite tricky to judge. Thus the routes as described are for opting out or opting in, depending on the reader's interest.

## Getting to Scotland

In addition to its internal ferry services to the islands and Shetland's Scandinavian connections, Scotland has direct car ferry links only with Northern Ireland, entering at Stranraer and Cairnryan in Galloway. Thus it is safe to assume that the huge majority of visitors to Scotland with cars will drive there from England. The M6 from the south is usually reckoned to be the quickest. On crossing the Border, this road deteriorates into the A74, an over-used dual carriageway at time of writing, though plans are afoot to upgrade it. Edinburgh-bound visitors are recommended to take the quieter A7 via Hawick.

Further east, the single-carriageway A68 (leaving the A1 south of Newcastle) crosses the Border at Carter Bar and provides perhaps the most spectacular entry into Scotland. Eastwards again, the single-carriageway A697, also leaving the A1, this time north of Newcastle, gives a gentle taste of rolling Border country after it arrives in Scotland at Coldstream. This is a fairly quiet, 'back door' route. The main eastern route, the A1, is still single carriageway in places north of Berwick-upon-Tweed (in medieval times one of Scotland's principal ports before a border change put it in England!). The A1 skirts the Southern Uplands through which the other routes pass. Edinburgh, though capital of Scotland, has no motorway connections with England; but, like Glasgow, it lies close to Scotland's own motorway system.

Allow, say, a very comfortable seven hours with stops to reach Edinburgh from the London area—but deduct up to two hours if the Borders are your first destination.

## Single-track Road Driving

Whereas driving in general is much the same as in the rest of the UK, Scotland still has some surviving single-track roads which demand a more considerate technique than is the norm. Blind bends or thick woodlands mean high average speeds can be maintained only by endangering other road users. In short—drive slowly and with care. However, the total mileage of single-track road drops with each succeeding year—for instance, you can reach Lochinver, in Sutherland, and even further, and never find yourself on one. Remember that passing places are definitely not for parking in, even if you think there is an eagle on the skyline and are fumbling for binoculars. Passing places should also be used for overtaking—let the other driver through as soon as you see him or her in your mirror. It might be the local doctor.

## Scottish Roads—Good and Bad

The routes described in this book try to avoid stretches of some of my least favourite roads. These include the A75 Gretna to Stranraer (heavy traffic to/from Ireland); A74 Gretna–to/from Glasgow (too much traffic on inadequate road); A929/A94 Dundee–Aberdeen via Forfar (part-dual, part-single carriageway—some drivers unable to distinguish differences between them; also fish-lorries dribble strange fluids on to windscreens of following vehicles). The A93 from Blairgowrie to the ski-slopes at Glenshee on a Sunday in winter can also be a frightening experience with much bad driving from over-eager young skiers.

More positively, many roads in Scotland are exhilarating and rewarding:

the road to Inverness from Fort Augustus by the east side of Loch Ness with endless views into the lonely hills of the Monadhliath; the much-improved A9 above Pitlochry, especially the high-level section through the Pass of Killiecrankie opening up a fast avenue to the north; the main road through Glencoe with gloomy grandeur on both sides; the Cairn o' Mount road from Banchory to Fettercairn high on the roof of the Grampians. These are just a few examples from a very wide choice.

## Accommodation

The Scottish Tourist Board was the first in the UK to introduce a qualitative element in its inspection scheme, to help take the guesswork out of booking accommodation in hotels, guest houses, bed-and-breakfasts and self-catering accommodation. (Caravan parks have their own scheme.) Briefly, establishments participating in STB's *classification* and *grading* scheme are visited and inspected for their range of facilities. A basic B&B might get the lowest *classification*, which is simply described as 'Listed', one slightly better-equipped might be awarded 'one crown' and so on, right up to top-class luxury hotels (or self-catering) which would be shown as 'five crowns'.

The interesting part, however, is the *grading* element, which assesses not the range of facilities, but their quality, as well as looking at harder-to-define factors such as ambience and friendliness. A 'five crown' hotel, for instance, would have a night porter. But if he was surly and unhelpful, then this would affect the grade of the hotel. Similarly a very basic B&B might be exceptionally clean and friendly. This also would affect the grade. The grade awarded depends on a wide range of factors but, in the final reckoning, is actually much more important than the crown classification. Grades range from 'Approved', which is (truthfully) fairly ordinary, through 'Commended', to 'Highly Commended'. Thus it is possible to find a 'Highly Commended', two-crown guest house and an 'Approved' four-crown hotel. This means that of its type, the guest house is probably much better value for money than the hotel. The message is, when booking accommodation, look closely at the grading, not the classification. This gives sound information on which to base your decisions.

Not every establishment is in the scheme—in fact, some very good places are not—but each one that participates is inspected annually. The Scottish Tourist Board's range of 'Where to Stay' guides show the classifications and gradings, so do the accommodation brochures and lists available from Scotland's area tourist boards. All tourist information centres also carry the information—as well as a full list of the criteria which are used in making the qualitative judgements.
On nearly all the routes, I have mentioned one or two possible places to stay.

## Useful Addresses

The statutory body charged with promoting tourism in Scotland is the **Scottish Tourist Board**, 23 Ravelston Terrace, Edinburgh EH4 3EU

(031 332 2433). It offers a range of helpful literature and you can find out more by writing to the above address or calling in person at the **Scottish Travel Centre**, 14 South St Andrew Street, Edinburgh (031 557 5522); the **Scottish Travel Centre**, 19 Cockspur Street, London, England (01 930 8661) or **Southwaite Tourist Information Centre**, strategically sited on the M6 just south of Carlisle.

In addition, within Scotland there are around 160 tourist information centres—look for the blue on white 'i' sign. They can not only advise on the details of the many places of interest but also help with just about any other enquiry, including accommodation and events. These information centres are run by a network of area tourist boards (or participating district councils) who also produce a wealth of literature. A full list of 'ATBs' is available from the Scottish Tourist Board. Remember that the number of tourist information centres open is greatly diminished in winter.

## Abbreviations

NTS     National Trust for Scotland (NB most properties open all year round)
OS      Ordnance Survey
RSPB    Royal Society for the Protection of Birds

## Tartan

Much of today's tartan is a hugely successful myth, created to satisfy a need for a suitably romantic image of Scotland. Certainly clansmen wore a long belted plaid, but they identified other clans and groups by badges. Hence the 'white cockade' of the 1745 Jacobite rebellion Specific 'clan tartan' is a successful marketing device of the 19C Scottish textile industry. Ironically, though the Highland clan system was ruthlessly dismantled after Culloden, the Gael has given all of Scotland its most potent symbol, adopted by Scots, Lowland and Highland, at home and overseas.

## The Scots Tongue

Grasping the nature of the languages or dialects of Scotland is crucial to understanding the nation's history. Today, Gaelic, the language of the Celts, is confined to the west, with its stronghold in the Western Isles. Once, say around the time of the Norman Conquest, it was spoken over much of the Lowlands. The evidence for it can be seen in a variety of surviving Lowland place names. With the arrival of Saxon settlers from the south, the original Celts were forced westwards into the Highlands and the clan system evolved, marked out as different in language as well as in values and social structure.

These Lowland 'sassenachs' (= Saxons, i.e. Lowland Scots or English undifferentiated) were Angles and Saxons who spoke a Northumbrian dialect, and originally settled between the Tweed and Forth in south-east

Scotland, before pushing northwards in the 12C and 13C. They brought with them a dialect already influenced by the Norse settlements established in northern England—and this Norse flavour continued to be very strong. The languages of Scotland were influenced by many other historical events, including the arrival of the refugee English royal family who fled into Scotland after the coming of the Normans in 1066. The English Princess Margaret married the Scottish King Malcolm Canmore.

Gradually, Norman influences also spread from the south, while medieval trading links with the Low Countries resulted in several borrowings from Dutch. Political and trading relationships with France also made their mark on the language of the Scots.

In short, Scotland eventually came to speak Gaelic only in the Highlands and a language in the Lowlands that by the 14C was usually called Inglis. By the end of the 15C it began to be called Scots—though its close links with the dialect of south of the Border meant that Scots poets were quite happy to borrow 'English' spellings for instance, especially under the influence of the writings of Chaucer. Scots, the language of Lowland Scotland, thus had an Anglo-Saxon origin, with influence from Norse, French, Dutch and even some Gaelic words. That is still so to this day.

The years 1460 to 1560 were its finest flowering as the language of literature and the speech of court. The invention of printing meant the adoption of many English conventions; the printing of the King James Bible, for instance, in English and not 'Scots' further helped reduce its religious status. The Union of the Crowns in 1603, when King James VI of Scotland packed his bags and left the Scottish court to become James I of England, meant the loss of social status for the Scots tongue. With the Union of Parliaments in 1707, English became the official language of administration and legislation.

The wonder is that either Gaelic or Scots survive at all. The clan system was ruthlessly dismantled after the Battle of Culloden in 1746. Highland emigration and clearances then took their toll. Yet, despite the enormous changes in the Highland way of life in the last 250 years, Gaelic is enjoying, perhaps, increasing attention in the Highlands—with the greatest concentration of Gaelic speakers in Scotland being in the Outer Hebrides.

As for Lowland Scots, though Ayrshire and the south-west have their own dialects, likewise Shetland which is much influenced by Norse, the heartlands probably lie in the north-east Lowlands. Here a rich dialect or language survives, mainly in a domestic context, spoken amongst ordinary folk in village, farm or local shop. Its greatest threat is from the media and from newcomers to the area who do not speak it. All Scottish dialect speakers tend to drift naturally into a form of standard English when addressing a non-dialect speaker, partly out of courtesy, partly from a long-instilled sense—quite wrong—that their language is a corrupt form of standard English instead of another branch of it, now differing from it only a little in grammar, quite a lot in vocabulary and a great deal in pronunciation.

However, even the Scots tongue is gaining a little in status as it begins to dawn on the native population that their linguistic heritage is increasingly under threat. Today, school children are probably not punished with the 'tawse' (leather belt) for speaking it within earshot of teachers intent on making their pupils ape the dialect of the Thames Valley which became standard English.

Here is a short glossary mostly of Lowland Scots, still used today, and Gaelic place names, very often found in an 'anglicised' form. Most of these words are in common currency and will be understood widely north of the Border, though a few are widespread only in Angus and Grampian.
*(Note: pronounce 'ch' in all cases as in Scottish 'loch'.)*

## Scots

| | |
|---|---|
| ashet (n) | large serving plate (cf. French *assiette*). Popularly quoted in 'Taste of Scotland' type cookery books as example of French influence in the Scots kitchen. |
| bairn (n) | child. |
| bield (n or v) | shelter (e.g. Bieldside near Aberdeen). |
| bool in the mou | literally 'marble in the mouth'. Wonderfully deflating phrase describing the attempts by Scots to adopt an upper-class accent; or descriptive of the accent itself, no matter who is using it. |
| bothy (n) | originally, accommodation for unmarried farmhands. Now, often basic shelter for hill-climbers. |
| burgh (n) | from 12C onwards, a Scottish town with trading rights granted from a higher authority (e.g. Royal Burgh, if granted by the king). |
| burn (n) | stream |
| ceilidh (n) | (Gaelic—but widely used) a gathering for musical entertainment. (Pronounce '*kay*-lay'.) |
| clan (n) | literally, in Gaelic, offspring or tribe. A former tribal or social structure of the Highlands, which involved families and extended families being under the protection of and prepared to defend their clan chief. |
| coup (v or n) | to upset, or a dump (cf. French). Like loup, to jump, and roup, an auction, pronounce with an 'ow' sound as in 'now'. |
| dreich (adj) | dull. (Of weather or a play at the Edinburgh Festival.) |
| dry-stane dykes (np) | literally, dry-stone walls (i.e. made without mortar). |
| gigot (n) | (of lamb) leg of lamb (from French *gigot*—cf. ashet above). |

| | |
|---|---|
| girn (v) | to cry and complain (as bairns sometimes do). |
| glen (n) | valley, usually U-shaped in profile, in the Scottish Highlands. |
| hirple (v) | to limp. (What you might do if improperly shod in the Scottish hills.) |
| howff (n) | shelter. (Sometimes a drinking-den, sometimes a rough hill shelter for climbers.) |
| kirk (n) | church, hence kirkyard—graveyard. |
| laird (n) | local landowner in (mainly Lowland) Scotland (cf. lord). |
| loch (n) | lake. |
| loon (n) | boy. |
| mercat (n) | market. Often in the form mercat cross, the symbolic centre-piece of a Scottish burgh. |
| muckle (adj) | big. |
| orra (adj) | spare and hence untidy or shabby. ('Orraman' as odd-job man/farmhand still to be seen in 'sits. vac.' column in some Scottish newspapers.) |
| policies (n) | the grounds or parkland of a mansion. |
| quine (n) | girl. |
| shargar (n) | smallest, stunted, 'runt of litter' (cf. Shergar, racehorse). |
| skyrie (adj) | garish. (Perhaps of a modern tartan design.) |
| sleekit (adj) | sly. |
| stravaig (v) | to wander, especially off the beaten track. (Much the best way to travel in Scotland.) |
| toun (n) | as well as simply town, also a hamlet or very small settlement (e.g. kirktoun round a church, fairmtoun by a farm). |
| yett | gate |

## Some Gaelic Elements in Scottish Place Names

| | |
|---|---|
| Aber ... | confluence or mouth of. (Early form of Gaelic, cf. Welsh.) |
| Alt/Auld ... | burn or stream |
| Bal ... | (G. *Bhaille* etc.): town or homestead (e.g. Ballater, Ballindalloch etc.). |
| Ben | (G. *Beinn* etc.): mountain. |
| Brae | (G. *Braigh*): upper part (e.g. Braemar, Braemore). |
| Corrie | (G. *Coire* etc.): glacial feature—rounded hollow or cirque on mountainside. |
| Drum ... | (G. *Druim*): ridge (e.g. Drumnadrochit). |
| Dubh | black. |
| Inver/Inbhir ... | as Aber, but later form of Gaelic. |
| Kil ... | (G. *Cille*) (usually) church (e.g. Kildonan, Kilmartin). |

| | |
|---|---|
| Linn | a pool (often below a waterfall). |
| More | great, large (Ben More, Braemore). |
| Strath | a broad valley (e.g. Strathspey, Strathmore). |

These are all commonly found in place names, sometimes for quite small features, as a glance at any Ordnance Survey 1:50,000 series will reveal.

# 1 SOUTHERN SCOTLAND

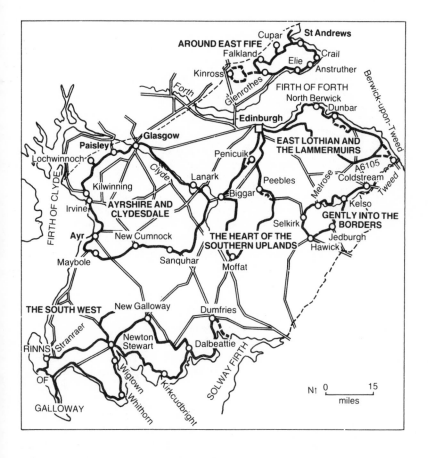

This section includes all of Scotland below its narrow waist, nipped by the estuaries of the Rivers Forth, Tay and Clyde. It takes in the long rolling hills and woollen towns of the Borders and the wild woods and moors of Galloway's uplands. Glasgow and Edinburgh may be the two largest cities in Scotland, but from both it is easy to find some attractive countryside.

9

East Lothian's beaches are about half an hour from Edinburgh, while across the Forth lie the neat farmlands and manicured golf courses of Fife. Equally close to Glasgow are the orchards of Clydesdale and the Clyde coast resorts.

## Gently into the Borders

*1–2 days/70 miles (112km)/from Coldstream*

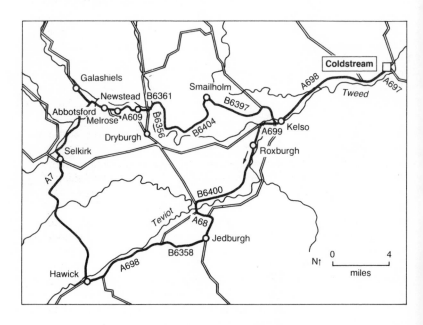

> O Caledonia! Stern and wild,
> Meet nurse for a poetic child!
> Land of brown heath and shaggy wood,
> Land of the mountain and the flood . . .
>
> from 'The Lay of the Last Minstrel',
> Sir Walter Scott

The Tweed Bridge on the south side of Coldstream marks the Border in this gentle introduction to Scotland. Though Edinburgh is only a little over an hour away, divert westwards across the well-tended Borders countryside. This is a route that takes in some fine views, as well as the panache of some of the stately homes which further embellish this well-tended stretch of Borders countryside. River valleys, with gently sloping fields, stitched together with a reasonably generous tree-cover, all set the scene.

The route visits the Borders towns, no two alike, each fiercely loyal to

10

its own rugby team. Also covered in the drive are the four great Border abbeys—Kelso, Jedburgh, Melrose and Dryburgh. The interpretative centre at Jedburgh Abbey is the key to understanding the role of these early religious foundations and the impact that they had not only in the religious life of Scotland but also on its industry and commerce. The growth of the great textile mills in many of the towns can be traced back to the early introduction of spinning techniques by the monks. The grazing grounds on open grassy hillslopes and the fast-running rivers as a source of power were other factors which, in turn, helped develop the Borders as the principal textile manufacturing area of Scotland. If you pass this way in early summer, check locally for the dates of the nearest Common Ridings. These great festivals and celebration of the horse are annual events. Selkirk claims its Common Riding to be the largest mounted gathering in Europe.

On A697 approaching **COLDSTREAM**, the **Tweed Bridge** of 1776 was once a place of safety for eloping couples from the south, rivalling the better-known Gretna Green, as the plaque on the wall of the nearby cottage and former toll house relates. (Scotland then had more accommodating marriage laws.) Today tidy and unassuming, Coldstream recalls in its local museum its other claim to fame, the regiment which has borne its name since 1659. As you leave the little town on the 'Scottish' side, still on A697, the signpost points right for **The Hirsel**. This is the estate of Lord Home, the former Prime Minister Sir Alec Douglas-Home. The grounds are open to visitors. There are craftworkers round a courtyard, a Homestead Museum, ornithologically interesting walks and brilliant rhododendrons all to detain you.

Take A698 to **KELSO**, enjoying views of the Tweed. Kelso town centre has an almost continental atmosphere—some have compared it to a Belgian market town—thanks to its broad paved square and mellowed buildings. Its early 12C **Abbey** is a tantalising fragment, destroyed, like the other Border abbeys, by the Earl of Hertford (1545) on the orders of England's King Henry VIII. (He was hoping to 'persuade' the Scots to let his young son, the Prince of Wales, marry the infant Mary Queen of Scots.) The local tourist information centre is close by the abbey, while round the corner is **Rennie's Bridge** (1803) built as a prototype for Old Waterloo Bridge in London (now demolished—though two lamp-posts were saved and now decorate Kelso's bridge!).

The bridge here also gives views across to **Floors Castle**, said to be the largest occupied house in Scotland. This property of the Duke of Roxburghe is open to the public. Take A699 out of Kelso, then take a minor road signed Roxburgh. The original Roxburgh Castle and its settlement, one of Scotland's earliest burghs, have all but disappeared. The village which you pass is a much later community.

Navigate, parallel to the River Teviot, by the Waterloo Monument, pencil-thin on the wide skyline ahead. Soon you will join B6400, right, and find the **Woodland Centre**. This is another Borders estate that welcomes visitors to walks and an Interpretative Centre on the various aspects of estate management. Greatly enlightened on rural ways, you should manage a light lunch here as well—there is a tea-room.

Swing south (left) on A68 to reach **JEDBURGH**. As the first town in Scotland on an old-established route, Jedburgh had the misfortune to lie in the path of invading Border armies and suffered in consequence. You may be reminded of this by the size of the car and coach park today. However, today's battalions of visitors are very well behaved and appreciate the comprehensively stocked tourist information centre overlooking the parking area.

Busy Jedburgh is the main interpretation point on the life of the great Border Abbeys, thanks to the comprehensive **Visitor Centre** adjacent to the shell of **Jedburgh Abbey** itself. Mary Queen of Scots was only one of a number of Scottish historic figures who have passed this way. As the Interpretation Centre at **Mary Queen of Scots House** relates, she, foolish lass, made an exhausting ride from Jedburgh to Hermitage Castle (about 20 miles/32km) and back in a day to see her wounded lover, Bothwell.

From Jedburgh take the road westwards (B6358/A698) for a glimpse of **HAWICK**, busiest and biggest of the Border towns. There is a good local museum in the well-laid-out **Wilton Park**, a choice of knitwear shops, and some inspiring views of blue hills hummocked to the horizon as you take A7 north to **SELKIRK**. This little town is the home of the bannock of the same name. Turn right at the foot of the hill to find the bakery which sells this wholesome fruit bun. Selkirk, too, has its historic association: courtroom of Sir Walter Scott; reconstructed ironmonger's shop in its local museum; statue to Mungo Park the Scottish explorer. Also, to the west, is the grand 19C house of **Bowhill**, with works by Canaletto, Gainsborough, Reynolds and Raeburn (to add a Scottish touch) all gracing the decor. For quality accommodation and meals in the Selkirk area, the **Philiphaugh Hotel** (0750 20747), beyond the town and over the Ettrick Water, is recommended.

Stay on A7 as it swings out of Selkirk, past the inevitable woollen mills, and soon over the Tweed again—glittering river vistas are a feature of most Borders drives. If you are still hunting for a jacket to match the sweater you bought earlier, then divert to workaday **GALASHIELS** with its textile shopping choice. The **Peter Anderson Woollen Mill** offers more than just a mill shop—it gives a comprehensive guide to the industry by way of its museum and exhibition on the growth of Galashiels, and offers tours of its manufacturing process. The textile theme—this time with live sheep amongst the exhibits—is found again at the **Border Wool Centre**, also near the town. Otherwise, the home of that great champion of a special brand of Scottishness, Sir Walter Scott, is tucked nearby at **Abbotsford**. In 1811, Scott bought a farm here, called Cartleyhole (really Clartyhole: clarty means muddy or dirty in Scots). Not surprisingly, Sir Walter renamed the property Abbotsford and entirely rebuilt it over the years. It is now a treasury of memorabilia, both of Scott himself and of relics of Scottish history, much of which he collected. His direct descendants still own the property.

**MELROSE** is minutes away by the A609 with another ruined 12C **Abbey**, glowing in warm red stone beneath the three tops of the Eildon Hills. Hertford's men also did their task well here, but some of the abbey's fine traceried stonework survives, as does some unusual carving, particularly that of a pig playing bagpipes, high in the roof. Next door is **Priorwood Gardens**, where the NTS specialises in flowers for drying and also old-fashioned apple varieties. Beyond the Abbey is, rather unexpectedly, a **Motor Museum**, while up the hill, under the former railway bridge (now a road bypass) and towards the golf course, is the path to the **Eildon Hills**, the Trimontium of the Romans who built a fort at nearby Newstead to guard the Border routes. (Though one of the very largest Roman sites in Scotland, little can be seen today.)

Train buffs should pay their respects to the now-restored and imposing Jacobean exterior of **Melrose Station**, now a crafts complex. The station is signed from the main square. On one level are a well-stocked crafts centre and restaurant, both of high quality, and upstairs at platform level a combined museum and railway modellers' shop, plus a gallery and craft workshops. The only trains to be seen are on the centre's model railway. The romance of the famous 'Waverley Route' clings on, though the main line, across the wild hills from Carlisle directly to Edinburgh, closed in 1969, leaving all of the Border towns and rural communities rail-less. Melrose, with its compact, triangular street layout, is a beguiling and peaceful place. As well as the Melrose Station restaurant, **Burts Hotel** (089682 2285) on Market Square is a listed building (1722) and serves a brisk and wholesome pub lunch.

Leave Melrose eastwards for the main A68 by way of B6361 (signed Newstead). You soon meet another reminder of those days of more relaxing transport. The Leaderfoot Viaduct, with its long-dead cross-country branch

formerly east-coast bound, spins a spidery elegance over river and road. The road goes under the viaduct, then past the road bridge to join A68. Turn left, cross the 'new' A68 bridge, then turn right immediately beyond to join a network of delightful 'back roads' which eventually thread through to Kelso. Signposting is good—follow them to B6356 and **Scott's View**, where the Tweed loops through a great harmony of field and wood with the landmark Eildons beyond. Scott often drove round by this view. Later, his own funeral cortège passed this way and the horses stopped at the spot as usual, of their own accord. Or so the romantic tale is told.

*Dryburgh Abbey*

13

*Mellerstain*

Continue on B6356, noting the right turn at the junction which leads on to the last of the four great abbeys on this route—and perhaps the most peaceful and atmospheric. In stately parkland, on a quiet riverside setting, the cloisters of **Dryburgh Abbey** complex are amongst the best preserved in Scotland, having survived the English King Henry's 'rough wooing', as the destructive episode was known. Scott himself is buried here. After visiting the Abbey, rejoin B6356, which leads on to a junction with B6404, signed for your next option, left, **Smailholm Tower**, which soon stands on your left, against the horizon and beyond open fields, ploughed red in spring. On a clear day, Smailholm offers one of the most outstanding panoramas to be enjoyed anywhere in the south of Scotland. This 16C fortified Border keep watches from high ground over a huge swathe of countryside, once troubled by reivers (cattle thieves) and warring expeditions. Yet there is no escape from the ubiquitous Sir Walter. Inside the tower is a most unwarlike exhibition of dolls and tapestries on the theme of his 'Minstrelsy of the Scottish Border'. He spent some of his childhood years at nearby Sandyknowe Farm.

A short but narrow road between 'dry-stane dykes' leads to Smailholm village, from where the attractive Adam mansion of **Mellerstain** is signed by way of B6397, left. Turning right returns you to Kelso and hence Coldstream.

## East Lothian and the Lammermuir Hills

*1 day/100 miles (160km)/from Edinburgh*

> The boat rocks at the Pier o Leith
> Fu' loud the wind blaws frae the Ferry
> The ship rides by the Berwick Law
> And I maun leave my bonny Mary.
>
> 'The Silver Tassie' (My Bonnie Mary),
> Robert Burns

The Lammermuirs, along with the Moorfoots and the Pentlands, are uplands which roughly mark the southern edge of the Lothians—the lands around the capital, Edinburgh. You can see parts of this long, broken line of hills from Edinburgh Castle battlements, or from Calton

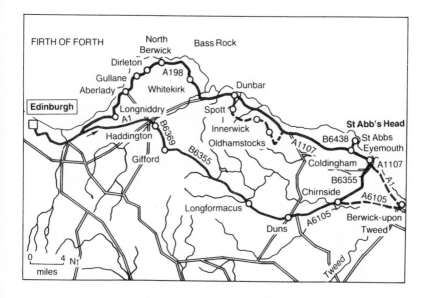

Hill, an even finer viewpoint. However, the best views of the Lammermuirs lie outside the city, from high points near the East Lothian coastline, such as the Berwick Law, which rises steeply behind the resort of North Berwick.

This route shows how easy it is to find attractive and peaceful countryside away from the hubbub and city-centre parking squabbles of Edinburgh. Though it starts from the capital, it could equally be enjoyed say, from Berwick-upon-Tweed, even if that attractive and historic town is on the wrong side of the Border!

**EDINBURGH** pop. 433,480    Tourist Information Centre: Waverley Market, Princes Street (031 557 1700). Capital of Scotland, divided into the Old Town, New Town and suburban spread. Originally a walled town built below its castle on the upper part of a rocky ramp sloping down from the Castle Rock to Holyrood Park, now the Old Town is usually taken to mean any part of the Castle-Holyrood Park link, whose main street is the famous Royal Mile. The New Town is that part of the city centre stretching several streets north of Princes Street, Scotland's most famous thoroughfare, which has outstanding views to the Castle. This dominates the city-centre and is a landmark (and navigational aid for first-time visitors).

For a flavour of Old Town life in former days, explore the 'closes' running like ribs off the backbone of the Royal Mile. Places of interest in the Old Town include, at the very top, the castle itself. Running downhill, the selection takes in the Scotch Whisky Heritage Centre, the Camera Obscura, a projected Edinburgh Story Visitor Centre, Gladstone's Land, Lady Stair's House, the High Kirk of St Giles, John Knox

House, The Museum of Childhood, Huntly House Museum and the Palace of Holyroodhouse.

The New Town post-1767 phase of building, beyond the confines of the Old Town, is noted for its neo-classical theme: stately buildings with 'palace-fronts' or otherwise elegant façades bringing a sense of order and spaciousness to the quieter streets of the area (that is, those which unlike Princes Street did not fall prey to later commercial developments). The Adam north façade of Charlotte Square is still one of Europe's finest examples of civic architecture. Catch the flavour of the age at the Georgian House at no. 7, the NTS's period piece. Alternatively you can enjoy New Town life by staying with **Edinburgh Holidays** (Mrs Sibbett 031 556 1078), an elegant and friendly B&B in a listed Georgian town house where Mr Sibbett plays bagpipes only on request. In a city which boasts the Edinburgh International Festival and fills to capacity every August, there is a wealth of accommodation of all kinds.

Such elegant colonnaded public works of the age, for example the National Gallery, or the miscellaneous collection of monuments on Calton Hill, earned Edinburgh the title of the Athens of the North. Edinburgh is well stocked with civic and private art galleries, plus the Royal Museums of Scotland. Beyond the immediate centre there are good shopping areas such as Stockbridge, Morningside or Bruntsfield, leafy walkways along the Water of Leith, plus other attractions: the outstanding Royal Botanic Gardens or, further out, the zoo and Lauriston Castle. Likewise on the edge are placid estuarine Cramond, and Colinton and Swanston, both with Robert Louis Stevenson associations. Visitors hankering for green spaces within walking distance of the centre can enjoy exploring the surprisingly wild landscapes of Holyrood Park— including Salisbury Crags and Duddingston Loch.

Opportunities for eating out, like accommodation, are very wide-ranging. For a treat you could enjoy the plasterwork and the elegant cuisine of the **Vintners Room** (031 554 6767/8423), a historic centre of Leith's wine trade. Much cheaper is the authentic Italian cuisine and friendly bustle of **La Lanterna** (031 226 3090) or the careful, clever and subtle flavours of the vegetarian Indian **Kalpna** (031 667 9890)—also excellent value.

Join the Edinburgh bypass eastbound (A1) to reach the former county town of **HADDINGTON**. The Georgian architecture in this elegant community can best be enjoyed on foot, giving enough time to note the detailing. Banks and private houses reflect the elegant, confident style, with arched fanlights and the occasional bold 'palace-front'. The Town House is by William Adam (1748, though enlarged 1830). Note, as you cross the Sidegate to reach the ancient Nungate footbridge, the wall plaque recalling the fearful heights of previous floods from the River Tyne. The medieval **Church of St Mary**, with its truncated spire, stands by the river.

Take B6369 south out of Haddington, noting on the way the sign (left) to **Lennoxlove House** which displays artefacts of Mary Queen of Scots.

Your route goes on to **GIFFORD**, with its 18C kirk and mercat cross and all the air of a contented, cosy backwater. Respectable, well-scrubbed, red-pantile-roofed East Lothian may well be Edinburgh's stockbroker belt—but the **Goblin Ha' Hotel** (062081 244) in Gifford does a wholesome afternoon tea even for ordinary folk.

Gifford lies on the very edge of the Lammermuirs. Climb out on B6355 to the south-east with mixed fields and woods giving way to rough heathery pasture and a surprisingly empty air for an area under an hour from the city. About 5 miles (8km) into the hills, look for a fork and a sign for Longformacus. Veer right.

This little road see-saws over attractive domed moors with croaking grouse and broad horizons. Then, beyond Longformacus, it leaves the Lammermuirs on a gentle descent towards Duns.

As the road drops down, the view across the Merse, the flood-plain of the River Tweed, is superb, with the broad whaleback of the Cheviot defining its southern boundary. **DUNS** is a compact market town, hardly overwhelming the visitor with points of interest, but certainly pleasant enough. The life of the Scots racing driver Jim Clark is recalled in his **Memorial Trophy Room**. The town was also the birthplace of John Duns Scotus, in 1266. This Franciscan divine and scholar is a little unkindly recalled in the word 'dunce'.

A6105 east from Duns leads to **Manderston**, another of the Borders' stately homes. This is amongst the youngest—an outstanding Edwardian confection, hardly modest with its dairy of marble and its unique silver staircase. Like most others in the area, it caters for visitors with its tearoom, shop and garden walks.

At Chirnside, scattered along a rise, take B6355 for Eyemouth. (If time is not pressing, you could continue on A6105 to Berwick-upon-Tweed, a town of great charm and interest, before heading north on A1/A1107 to reach Eyemouth.) At **EYEMOUTH**, the character of the route changes, with the return journey an exploration of the Berwickshire and East Lothian coastline. Eyemouth retains an active fishery, with working craft picturesquely tied up at weekends. Its **Museum**, in Market Place just behind the water-front, tells the tale of the great East Coast fishing disaster of 1881, when 129 Eyemouth men were lost.

Skirt Coldingham Bay on A1107, taking B6438 (right) for **ST ABBS**. Unless you are a sub-aqua enthusiast, the chief attraction of the little coastal village is its impressive sea-cliffs (**Scottish Wildlife Trust Reserve**) to the north-west. There is an 'official' car park at Northfield farm with a nearby visitor centre, toilets and tea-room with fresh home baking. Disabled drivers can take their cars another mile to the cliff-top lighthouse, from where it is a few moments to the impressive cliffs. Snowstorms of kittiwakes and rock shelves stacked with guillemots and razorbills make this one of the most impressive wildlife spectacles to be seen anywhere in the south of Scotland.

Return to the quiet A1107 at Coldingham and follow it north-west. About 6 miles (10km) further on, across the levels of Coldingham Moor, look for woodland hard by the road on your left (marked Old Cambus

Wood on OS maps). At the far end of the wood a track goes right, past a mast. If the weather is warm, the unfenced roadside makes an excellent picnic spot with wide views over the East Lothian coast.

A1107 joins A1—turn right to continue your route to **DUNBAR**, later signed off right. [If the single-minded whizz of Edinburgh-bound traffic is not to your liking, there is a network of unclassified roads between A1 and the edge of the Lammermuirs. Driving is a delight here, by way of Oldhamstocks, Innerwick and Spott, to Dunbar.]

This ancient burgh, despite its pleasantly faded air of a seaside resort that has formerly known great popularity, once played an important part in Scottish history and was one of many burned by the English Earl of Hertford in the episode of the 'rough wooing' (see Scottish history section). Amongst its many notable figures is, almost inevitably, Mary Queen of Scots, who was abducted by the Earl of Bothwell and brought to the castle here. It is now only a gaunt fragment, thanks partly to Oliver Cromwell in the following century who defeated the Royalist forces here in 1650, then used the already ruined castle stonework in building a harbour. Along the High Street, note the 17C Renaissance-flavoured **Town House and Tolbooth**, once the heart of the old burgh. There is also some fine 18C work in the town.

**Belhaven Bay**, with its wide-open sands (access from A1087), lies westwards. The long sandy shores in turn become part of the **John Muir Country Park**, which takes in the estuary of the River Tyne, a picturesque rocky shoreline, yet more high-grade sands, as well as the mixed woodlands of Tyninghame. (John Muir was a Dunbar lad who in early life emigrated with his family to the USA. He later founded their national parks system, including the famous Yosemite.) Access to the park can also be had from A198 (right) off the A1, 3 miles (5km) west, and A198 is also your turning for the final leg of the route.

At **Whitekirk**, the red sandstone church with its square Norman tower is built on a site dating back to the 6C. Look for the surviving tithe barn, in the field behind it. Only a few minutes further on, **Tantallon Castle** can be seen plainly across the level fields—a grim and battered curtain-wall squatly defending a headland. This was a Douglas stronghold and if you have the head for it, the battlements give outstanding views of the East Lothian countryside, rolling out to the Lammermuir edge.

A198, which has been slightly disorientatingly running north, now swings sharply west along the coast for North Berwick, marked by the unmistakable cone of the Berwick Law behind. Another of these strange volcanic plugs lies offshore—the **Bass Rock**, which you can sail round on an excursion from North Berwick's harbour and enjoy the gannet colonies. As for **NORTH BERWICK** itself, it is a 'Sunday afternoon' sort of place, where sailboards, crimplene cardigans and dribbly ice-cream meet and happily mingle. Its prevailing sound is wind-rung rigging jangling against metal masts.

East Lothian's golf courses seem to fill every available links space.

Yellow beaches run towards **Yellowcraigs**, with its choice of shore walks, signed from the village of **DIRLETON**, off A198. Dirleton's mellowed 12C **Castle** ruins peep over a wall and on to a curiously English-style village green. Nearby is the **Open Arms** (062085 241), a particularly welcoming hotel, with beguilingly deep sofas. (Anywhere from Dunbar westwards is within easy striking distance of Edinburgh, if you are considering staying out of town, say at Festival time.)

Continuing west, **GULLANE** is very respectable and liable to caddy-car jams. The Open Championship course at Muirfield is nearby, overlooked by the Sir Edwin Lutyens-designed mansion of **Greywalls** (0620 842144). This hotel has outstanding, though not inexpensive, cuisine. Gullane's beach is a popular attraction. Behind it are swathes of sea-buckthorn, a glaucous shrub with bright red autumn berries, usually in turn festooned with fieldfares and redwings, off-season thrush-family visitors from Scandinavia.

Though there is a growing sense of coastal commuter suburb (about half an hour from Edinburgh), **Aberlady Bay Nature Reserve**, only minutes to the west, offers muddy delights for the birdwatcher. Finally, beyond Aberlady, A198 leaves the coast for Longniddry (good pub lunches at the **Longniddry Inn**) and, after 4 miles (6km), joins the A1 and the bypass on the edge of the city.


# The Heart of the Southern Uplands

*1–2 days/95 miles (152km)/from Edinburgh*

> *Then issuing forth one giant wave*
> *And wheeling round the giant's grave*
> *White as the snowy charger's tail,*
> *Drives down the pass of Moffatdale.*

'Marmion'
Sir Walter Scott

Scott's description of the Grey Mare's Tail waterfall is only one of a number of landscape features woven into the poet's work which this excursion passes. These include Roslin and its castle as described in 'The Lay of the Last Minstrel'. Another theme is the growth of the great River Tweed, which rises, according to a roadside notice, in a high sedgy bowl in the Tweeddale Hills. This excursion passes the spot, but meets the Tweed first as a full-scale river rolling by Peebles, one of the most attractive of communities and a former county town. You will also journey into a sometimes overlooked area, away west from the concentration of the major Borders towns, yet with easy access from both Edinburgh and Glasgow. Though Moffat is the turning point of this out-and-back route, there are cross-country options which could shorten it to an easy day.

Pick up the A701 (Liberton Road) on your route southwards out of

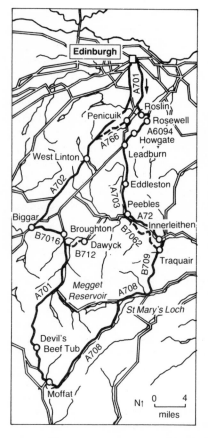

**EDINBURGH** (see p. 15). As (see p. 15) you leave the city boundary, note the Hillend Ski Slope—the largest artificial ski run in Britain—conspicuous on the north slope of the Pentlands, across the fields on your right. At the former mining community of Bilston, go left for **Rosslyn Chapel** (signed Roslin B7006). Look for further signs which will lead you to the Chapel itself. This extraordinary 15C conception by Sir William Sinclair, dedicated to St Matthew in 1450, displays the finest stone carving to be found anywhere in Scotland. It was intended to be cruciform, but only the choir was ever completed. Its stonework is encrusted with elaborate devices—human and animal figures, foliage and decorations. Rosslyn Castle below is private.

Rosslyn Chapel can be the start of a number of (mainly unofficial) excursions on foot, through the wooded Roslin Glen nearby from which half-hidden Hawthornden Castle can be glimpsed, once the home of the Scots poet William Drummond (1585–1649). At the west end of the village of Roslin, take a steeply descending road, B7003, across the sylvan glen, turning right at the mining village of Rosewell on to A6094. Then enjoy an 'arm's-length' view of the Pentland Hills arching along the skyline on your right. Turn left at Howgate.

At the Leadburn crossroads, take A703 left for Peebles, with the rounded Moorfoot Hills soon looming ahead. A little way beyond Eddleston, look for a sign to the **Cringletie House Hotel** (07213 233). This mansion of 1861 by David Bryce, stands in its own grounds, hidden from the main road. Its walled garden produces many fresh ingredients and the hotel has a good reputation for its food while managing to stay friendly and informal. A very relaxing way of route planning is to linger over post-lunch coffee served in a mellow, dark panelled lounge, while looking down the valley of the Eddleston Water to Peebles.

**PEEBLES**, well within popular commuting distance of the capital, is a well-mannered sort of place, its native population swelled in recent years by newcomers, beguiled by its rural charms, even though the streets fill with day-trip strollers in season. If the gentle bustle is not to your taste, then the town has a riverside park, which leads on to an upstream walk to

*Rosslyn Chapel*

**Neidpath Castle**, on a picture postcard bluff above the glinting Tweed waters. Peebles also has an unusual **Museum of Ornamental Plasterwork**.

From Peebles, take the main A72 eastwards along the river-valley to Innerleithen, with a NTS shop in a preserved former printing works. Beyond this textile community is another: Walkerburn, home of the **Scottish Museum of Woollen Textiles**, an interesting display which is entered only after running the risk of temptation by way of 'sale rails' and special offers in the inevitable woollen shop.

As an alternative, from Peebles cross the Tweed bridge, noting the ornate dolphin lamp-posts, going left on B7062 which follows the river downstream to **Traquair House**. This is the home of the Maxwell-Stuarts and claims to be Scotland's oldest continually occupied house. It dates back to the 10C and in the intervening years has been visited by 27 kings and queens.

The owners for long supported the Catholic Stuart (previously Stewart) monarchs of Scotland. When Prince Charles Edward Stuart visited in 1745, gathering support in the final rebellious campaign against the Protestant Hanoverians, Traquair's gates were closed on his departure. A vow was made never to open them till a Stuart gained the throne. Thus they have been closed ever since. To get round the inconvenience, Traquair now has two main drives in parallel. Charming and idiosyncratic—and with a good tea-room—Traquair is a delight.

From Innerleithen or Traquair, take B709, through sheep-cropped hills south to A708, turning right and on past St Mary's Loch to the **Grey Mare's Tail**. This spectacular waterfall spills from a hanging valley down to a geography text-book U-shaped valley. It is in the care of the NTS. There are two paths to see the falls, high- or low-level. You should be well-shod if taking exercise on the higher of the two, which leads eventually to Loch Skeen and the great domed hill called White Coomb, one of the highest points in the Southern Uplands, comparing in height with many a Highland peak (2,696ft/822m).

Follow the Moffat Water, winding between the green walls of the glacial valley, all the way to the wool town of **MOFFAT**. Look for the Colvin Fountain with ram statue in the town square, as another reminder of the area's preoccupation with sheep. The town once gained minor prominence as a spa resort, a tale told in the local **Museum**. Otherwise, Moffat has a reasonable shopping choice, including a good range of woollens at **Moffat Weavers**, which sounds homespun but is part of a large retailing operation, and you should be able to find afternoon tea.

Your return route, on A701, climbs steadily out of the town, with a valley deepening on the right. The head of this valley becomes the **Devil's Beef Tub**—more evidence of Border glaciers at work. Sir Walter Scott in 'Redgauntlet' describes it as a 'deep, black, blackguard-looking hole of an ·abyss'. This may be a literary overstatement for this steep-sided amphitheatre in the hills.

Beyond a high and lonely watershed, around which the slopes are squared and scarred by uncouth forestry blocks, a little sign points out the source of the Tweed. Further down, the **Border Collie and Shepherd Centre** at Tweedhopefoot, near Tweedsmuir, gives sheepdog displays. The dogs also herd ducks, by way of a demonstration, though one may get the impression that the well-rehearsed ducks would huddle together and scurry into their pens even without the dogs!

Before reaching Broughton, B712 joins on the right. The botanically minded should divert here for **Dawyck Botanic Gardens** (pronounced 'doyk', to rhyme almost with Hawick). This outstation of the Royal Botanic Garden in Edinburgh is a peaceful, secluded spot, much appreciated by the tall conifers sheltering unusual rhododendrons and other shrubs. (Try to visit in May/June if possible and bring plenty of colour film for the woodland walks.)

The main A701 continues to Broughton through pleasant upland variety with conifer copse, domed hills and with the young Tweed swinging briskly down—still more than 70 miles (112km) (as the salmon swims) from its estuary. At Broughton there is a museum, the **John Buchan Centre**, which tells the story of this now somewhat neglected author, the first Lord Tweedsmuir, perhaps best known for *The 39 Steps*. Divert westward here on B7016 signed for Biggar.

**BIGGAR** is of interest out of all proportion to its size. Midway from Edinburgh and Glasgow, with the headwaters of Clyde, flowing west, and Tweed, flowing east, the community is certainly not a faceless dormitory. Perhaps its location, far enough away from the sprawl of the Central Lowlands, yet not lost within bleak hills, helps it retain its own vigorous character. It also has an extraordinary range of attractions for visitors. These include a **puppet theatre**; also the **Gladstone Court Museum** with reconstructed shops and displays of local life; **Greenhill Covenanters House** which is a reminder that the lonely hills around were the scene of religious strife in the 17C; **Moat Park Heritage Centre**, which gives another insight into life around Clydesdale; also the local kirk is notable—a collegiate church of 1545. Finally, as an experience for all the senses, Biggar also boasts Scotland's only surviving **town gasworks**, preserved as one of the more eccentric, but very worthwhile, of the nation's scheduled ancient monuments. Visitors can relive the gassy smells of yesteryear!

The return to Edinburgh is by the A702. This route gives very fine views of the long slopes of the Pentland Hills, in places only a field's length from the road. There is easy access to these windy heights from points near Edinburgh such as **Nine Mile Burn** and **Flotterstone**. Both these places have pubs catering for walkers. However, further to the south and just off A702, the **Old Bakehouse Tea-room** (0968 60564) at West Linton offers outstanding afternoon teas, served by young lasses with white pinafores, entirely in keeping with their traditional surroundings. Finally, within a few minutes of the city boundary, **Edinburgh Crystal Visitor Centre** in the dormitory town of Penicuik welcomes visitors intent on glittering glassware purchases.

## Around East Fife

*1 day/(up to) 90 miles (144km)/from St Andrews*

*Oh we cast oor nets in Largo Bay and fishes we caught nine,*
*We had three tae bile and three tae fry and three tae bait the line.*
'The Boatie Rows'—traditional

Most visitors who go to Fife head straight for St Andrews, attracted by the golf, the colourful setting of this university and former ecclesiastical centre—and, perhaps, the unusually wide choice of designer shops. St Andrews has Scotland's oldest university (1410) and the town was for centuries the focus of Scotland's religious life. However, Fife also has much of interest in its well-tended hinterland. The 'far east' of Fife almost completely avoided the kind of industrial developments which grew up around the coalfields of west or central Fife. This route includes some rural byways well off the direct track and takes in some of north-east Fife's characterful countryside communities. Lush hedgerows, bountiful grain-fields and the sparkle of the sea, glimpsed across green countryside—Fife offers a most unusual ambience very far removed from the craggy stereo-type of Scotland.

There is also another aspect of Fife to be discovered. Like many other parts of the eastern Lowlands, Fife once had strong trading links with nations across the North Sea. From St Andrews right round to Kincardine, well up the Forth estuary, medieval merchants sent their vessels across the North Sea, dealing in wool, coal, spices, claret, herring, iron ore and many other commodities. (The Scottish Nationalists' slogan of 'Scotland in Europe' curiously echoes these endeavours).

The Low Countries links are very obviously recalled in the sport of golf, brought across the sea from Holland. From a crude pastime played, perhaps, with stick, round stone and several rabbit-holes in the cropped coastal turf, it has become a world-wide sport with St Andrews as its 'spiritual home'. Visitors less enamoured with birdies and bogies can enjoy instead the Dutch flavour in the architecture of the 'East Neuk' fishing villages, where tolbooth and town house, red pantiles and white crow-stepped gables recall those earlier times.

With its towers and romantic spires against calm skies over the North Sea, **ST ANDREWS**, the old ecclesiastical capital, is unmistakable. Nowhere else offers this strange mix of well-heeled golfing hotels, swish designer shops and mellow university precincts with upmarket students. Expensively clad golfing widows, extrovertly clad students, day trippers and the local folk all bustle together in the busy streets, in a historic setting which includes a fragmentary **cathedral**, once the largest in Scotland, a picturesque, tiny harbour, the only surviving town gate in a Scottish burgh, a ruined **castle** and an overall air of confidence and elitism, at least on the main streets. This interesting blend of attractions has been further enhanced by the opening of the **St Andrews Sea Life Centre**. There is a very large choice of places to eat, at all price ranges. **Brambles Restaurant** (0334 75380), in College Street near the Market Street fountain, serves relaxed, bistro-style food and home baking. Like many other St Andrews eating places within the student budget, there is much less background braying outside term-time.

Though there is much of interest in the town, including beaches above and below it, take A91 north-westwards. A few minutes later, at Guard-

*St Andrews Cathedral*

bridge, go right on A919, signed **LEUCHARS**. This little community has a superb **Norman church**, with chancel and apse dating from the early 13C. The pleasing patterns of its arcaded decoration are well set off by the church's position on a little mound. North of Leuchars an unclassified road (tricky to find—go past the school) sets off across the level fields. In less than 2 miles (3km), the **Tentsmuir Forest** is signed right. This well-established plantation shelters a superb sandy beach, long enough to leave the dog-walkers far behind and ideal for picnics.

Retrace your route to A91 at Guardbridge, going left (towards St Andrews) then very shortly right, signed Strathkinness, another unclassified road. Go right at the crossroads as you enter the village. [As an optional extension, just south of the peaceful little village, beyond a second crossroads, is a walk to **Magus Muir**. A belt of trees ahead seen from the village shows the position. A monument marks the scene of the murder of Archbishop Sharp of St Andrews by Covenanting fanatics in 1679—now the mixed woodland is appreciated by local wildlife.] However, if exercise is not required, the right turn before the village becomes a peaceful little road rolling through the tranquil Fife field patchwork. After 3 miles (5km), stop for a moment at **Dairsie Bridge**, seen on the immediate right, a triple-arched 450-year-old structure, under which the Eden flows. The countryside around seems the very essence of rural Fife. On the skyline is Dairsie Church, its exterior practically unchanged since the early 17C, while the ruins of Dairsie Castle standing starkly among the trees nearby add further atmosphere.

Do not cross the bridge but veer left towards Kemback, beyond which is the almost out of place **Dura Den**. The Ceres Burn, a tributary of the Eden, flows through this Highland glen in miniature, with its well-clad slopes, waterfalls and oddly moulded sandstone cliffs. The road emerges at Pitscottie. Go left and right to find B939 for **CERES**. (Read the road signs carefully or you will end up in Cupar!) Yet another tranquil overlooked village, Ceres offers the **Fife Folk Museum**, which reflects its essentially rural preoccupations. Look also for the Provost, a 17C jolly carved figure, complete with mug of ale, who sits in a niche opposite the road signed right for Hill of Tarvit. (A provost is a Scottish mayor.)

Follow signs for **Hill of Tarvit House**, only a mile or two west of Ceres. This late 17C mansion was totally remodelled in Edwardian times by the great Scottish architect, Sir Robert Lorimer. It offers a fine collection of paintings, furniture and tapestries (as well as a good cup of tea in the summer season). There is also a hilltop walk for the energetic.

From Hill of Tarvit, the option is to turn right on to A916 for **CUPAR**, a bustling market town just to the north. In the town, up a side alley, you can discover **Ostlers Close** (0334 55574) a small and friendly restaurant with a Scottish flavour. Otherwise follow the A916 briefly southwards (left) to Craigrothie, taking a right turn just beyond the village, signed Chance Inn. This little road runs along a green and wooded hill-slope, giving glimpses and longer views of the Howe of Fife, the well-cultivated open river-valley of the Eden. (Howe is Scots for hollow.) This rich agricultural area was once a poor and badly drained stretch of marsh and forest—which is why Fife was traditionally described as a 'beggar's mantle fringed with gold'. Fife now has a higher proportion of arable land than any other Scottish county.

Stay on the high ground by going firstly, right at a T-junction, then straight across at crossroads with derelict quarry buildings. The best views, which include the Lomond Hills ahead, are from a layby, about a mile further. This little road runs for a further 2 miles (3km) to a junction in a conifer plantation. Go right to drop off the gentle ridge, crossing A92 to reach Freuchie. Go straight through Freuchie, taking B936 for **FALKLAND**.

Tucked below the Lomond Hills, this red-roofed community grew up round the ancient hunting lodge of the Stewart monarchs, the surviving **Falkland Palace**. Its 16C façade dominates the main street. There are gardens and a *jeu quarre*, or royal tennis court, as part of the Palace complex. It is claimed that this court is the oldest in the UK. It was built for James V in 1539 and is still in regular use. Also within this attractive village are some atmospheric 17C and 18C buildings and antique and craft shops, well accustomed to a fast throughput of visitors.

Leave Falkland in a westerly direction by going past the antique shop at the far end of the square then bear left, signed Leslie and Craigmead. This minor road leads steeply up and over the Lomond Hills, an island of moors and pasture with gentler rural Fife eastwards and the more industrial landscapes on the other side. There are fine views of the Forth Valley as the road then makes a gentle descent from the twin humps of the East and West Lomonds. (These little peaks of 1394ft and 1713ft (432m and 531m), respectively, are conspicuous out of all proportion to their size. They can, for instance, be seen from the top of the chairlift at Glenshee in the Grampians.) You eventually reach the main street of workaday Leslie.

[The route at this point has an option to explore the environs of **Loch Leven**, one of Scotland's largest Lowland lochs, covering an area of more than 5sq. miles (13sq. km). To reach it, go right at Leslie along A911, cross the River Leven bridge, and continue west to B9097 which swings right then along the south shore of Loch Leven.

With Benarty Hill rising on your left, and the loch below on the right, look for the sign to indicate the RSPB's **Vane Farm Visitor Centre**. This is the best way to see the loch—either from the deluxe viewing conditions of the centre, complete with high-powered binoculars or, more energetically, by following the nature trail on to the rough moor above. You can easily drive all round the loch, taking in **KINROSS**, departure point for the ferry to **Loch Leven Castle**, with its romantic tale of Mary Queen of Scots' escape from island imprisonment there. Kinross also has mill shops while **Portcullis Antiques** is a rare find: an antiques business both friendly and fairly priced. Then retrace your route to Leslie.]

If time is pressing, from Leslie go left to follow the main A911 eastwards through less interesting landscapes, clipping the edge of the new town of Glenrothes and heading towards the coast to join A915 at Windygates. Return to the land of well-manicured golf courses at Lundin Links and Lower Largo.

**LOWER LARGO** is associated with Robinson Crusoe or, more accurately, his prototype, Alexander Selkirk, marooned for four years until 1709 on the island of Juan Fernandez in the South Pacific. There is a fine beach here, on the broad sweep of Largo Bay. At Upper Largo, go straight through, shortly to fork right on A917 for Elie. This road passes close to the attractive village of **KILCONQUHAR**, set in the midst of open woods and barley fields by a loch of the same name—idiosyncratically pronounced 'kinneyeuchar' with the usual Scots 'ch' sound.

A mile beyond, A917 returns to the coast at the twin resorts of **ELIE** and **EARLSFERRY**, neat and quiet places, where sailboard enthusiasts trudge dripping up the lanes from the shallow, sheltered harbour partly formed by an inshore island. Further east, the road goes on to **ST MONANS**, with the landmark of the **Auld Kirk**, on the very edge of the sea, as a reminder of this town's long involvement with its local fishery. Inside today's church, built on a site founded perhaps as early as AD400, there is an ornate model of a full-rigged sailing ship. Further evidence of seafaring activities can be seen by strolling around the harbour, where the flicker of the welder's torch and the clunk of adzes are a reminder of the long tradition of boat repairing and building.

Further along this fine coastline, **PITTENWEEM** is much appreciated by photographers of the 'wobbly mast reflections and orange net-float close-ups' school of photography. Certainly, it is a picturesque place. The National Trust for Scotland is among a number of conservation bodies who have been at work here, renewing the fabric of many sturdy fisher houses of the 17C and 18C. These now gleam crisply white with crow-steps, forestairs, red pantiles and carved lintels all adding authentic touches. There is also an active fishmarket here, at the centre of the East Fife fishery. Pittenweem is, in Gaelic, the 'place of the cave' and a cave survives, up a side alley by the waterfront. This is the **Shrine of St Fillan**, where a 7C missionary lived.

By way of a change from maritime matters, you can divert inland from Pittenweem (or St Monans) to visit **Kellie Castle**. Take the unclassified road left (north), out of Pittenweem, going left where it joins B9171. Kellie Castle dates from the 16/17C and was restored by Professor James

*Scottish Fisheries Museum, Anstruther*

Lorimer in the 19C. The interiors are impressive, but its charm lies in its 4-acre walled garden, a secluded, scented place of lavender and roses.

Back on the main A917, the maritime theme dominates the East Neuk communities. Next on the road is **ANSTRUTHER**. This is a substantial settlement with a large harbour and the flavour of a traditional resort with its forgivably garish buckets and spades festooning the equally brightly painted souvenir shops. A cheerful sea-breezy place, Anstruther is also the home of the **Scottish Fisheries Museum**, housed in a 16–19C complex of buildings known as St Ayles. Here, artefacts, documents, photographs and paintings, as well as eerily realistic tableaux, capture the former hardships in the lives of the Scottish fisherfolk. There is also an aquarium section which children will enjoy. Anstruther boasts an outstanding restaurant: **The Cellar** (0333 310378)—small and candle-lit as its name suggests and you must book in advance—but well worth tracking down for its careful, subtle presentation of top quality seafood.

All of these East Neuk communities are threaded together along the glittering sea-edge (perhaps it is a quality of the light streaming onshore along the south-facing coastline). It is only 4 miles (6km) to the most easterly of them, **CRAIL**, thought by some to be the most attractive of all. This early Royal Burgh (1310) was for long involved in the European trade—but its picturesque tiny harbour is a reminder of the small scale of those medieval trading vessels.

The status of Royal Burgh, granted by the Scottish king, gave a community trading rights and privileges, though some of the revenue found its way into the monarch's coffers. Surviving elements of these early burghs are seen all over Scotland, but Crail is a good example. Its mercat cross, though not in its original site, survives with its shaft 17C or earlier. The Marketgate (gate=street) has a number of 17/18C former merchants' houses as well as a tolbooth or toll house, 16C with later additions. Its sturdy, foursquare tower houses a bell with a Dutch inscription, cast in 1520. Part of the complex is now **Crail Museum and Heritage Centre**, which sheds further light on this old-established community.

The main road swings north-west and Fife shrinks towards the eastern tip, Fife Ness, haunt of birdwatchers during the spring and autumn migrations but otherwise a slight anticlimax—a stretch of low rocks and sand with, inevitably, a golf course and hotel. The coastline up to St Andrews is relatively unspoilt without reaching over-dramatic heights. There is a continuous coastal walk. One of the main access points is **Cambo**, part country park, part farm conversion into countryside interpretation centre on an estate with a good variety of habitat (and a tearoom!) plus farm animals of the suitably cuddly variety.

Nearby is **KINGSBARNS**, with another popular beach. The main road then runs on to St Andrews, giving fine town views from a gentle rise, with a backdrop of the hills of Angus.

# Ayrshire and Clydesdale

*2 days/140 miles (224km)/from Glasgow*

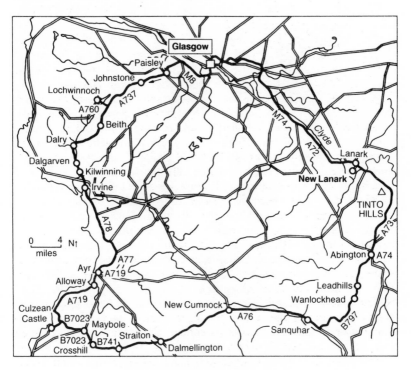

> *Oft hae I roved by bonnie Doon,*
> *To see the rose and woodbine twine;*
> *And ilka bird sang o its love,*
> *And fondly sae did I o mine.*

'The Banks o' Doon'
Robert Burns

This tour is an unusual blend of industrial heritage and rural settings. Much of it is in the old county of Ayr, strongly associated with the poet Robert Burns, where green pasture and rich feeding for plump dairy cattle are set against a background of mostly vanished industrial activity in which seams of coal and iron played their part. Further contrasts can be found when the route circles inland to lose lush pastures for upland heath on the way towards Clydesdale. Having looked at textiles, coal, iron, milling and shipbuilding, you can discover the story of lead mining in the highest community in Scotland, then the unique venture of New Lanark, a model spinning community.

This round trip can just about be done in a day, but really needs at least two if more than just a few of the venues described are to be thoroughly explored. Remember that local tourist information centres will help with accommodation.

**GLASGOW** pop. 765,000   Tourist Information Centre: 35 St Vincent Place (041 227 4800). Scotland's largest city, now making a substantial impact on Scottish tourism by a self-confident promotion of its new image. Probably has the finest Victorian city-centre buildings of any UK city and thus well worth seeing for this reason alone—outstanding examples include the Italian-inspired City Chambers, the Venetian Gothic Stock Exchange or the dignified neo-classicism of the former Royal Exchange (Stirling's Library). Has in addition an excellent choice of museums and galleries, including one of the UK's finest civic collections in the Kelvingrove Art Gallery and Museum. The city's Charles Rennie Mackintosh associations are also worth pursuing, starting with the Hunterian Art Gallery's reconstructed Mackintosh interiors.

In addition to the best shopping choice in Scotland, a rich cultural life aided by the fact that major 'cultural organisations' such as Scottish Opera, Scottish Ballet and the Scottish National Orchestra have their headquarters here, Glasgow offers a wide range of accommodation and cuisine. These include the sumptuous **One Devonshire Gardens** (041 339 2001) and the popular **Ubiquitous Chip** (041 334 5007).

Take the M8 west from Glasgow city centre and exit for **PAISLEY** (junction 27 or 29). Follow town centre signs. Paisley (pop. 85,000) is not the first place which springs to mind as a visitor destination but it is a town of great interest. **Paisley Abbey**, conspicuous in the centre, was founded in 1163. Burned by King Edward of England in 1307, rebuilding started later in the century, though much of the work is 15C. Subsequently, the building stood roofless from the 16C onwards, except for the nave which continued as the parish church. Now the whole building has been restored and is in use.

Weaving started as an ancillary activity round the abbey but grew to dominate the town by Victorian times. The teardrop-shaped 'Paisley pattern' on the town's famous shawls was brought to Scotland on shawls woven in Kashmir—it is thought to be an ancient 'symbol of life' originating in Indo-European cultures! The full story of Paisley's involvement in

*Paisley shawl*

the weaving industry is told in an excellent display at the **Paisley Museum and Art Gallery**—Britain's first municipally run museum (1871)—with its superb shawl collection. Another unusual feature is the **Coats Observatory** on the hill above, like the museum a gift from the Coats family, a famous name in cotton thread and benefactors to the town.

Take care while leaving Paisley. Follow signs for A760 Largs or Johnstone, or A761 Bridge of Weir until signs for your road, A737, appear. Beyond the undistinguished town of Johnstone—(go left, not right for the town centre, at a Y-junction) the countryside quite suddenly greens up with permanent pasture which is a feature of Ayrshire, the old county lying ahead. Soon after, with Castle Semple Loch on your right, divert a short way on to the A760 signed for Largs, to visit the RSPB's **Lochwinnoch Visitor Centre** (closed Thursdays). The centre has a viewing tower—with more hides nearer the water—and display area with a changing programme of exhibitions and information on the wildlife of the loch (great crested grebes a summer speciality plus up to 60 other breeding species and perhaps a resident otter or two). There are also RSPB goods for sale and a (weekend afternoon) tea-shop.

Return to A737, continuing past Beith and skirting Dalry, where you must watch the signs carefully—if you can see any—for Kilwinning. All the way along this part of the route the landscape is bright green pasture with thin stands of trees and hawthorn hedges—dairy country.

Before you reach Kilwinning, look closely for a 'thistle' sign taking you left for one of the most pleasing attractions on the drive. **Dalgarven Mill** is a working water-mill which also houses the **Museum of Ayrshire Country Life and Costume Collection**. Robert and Moira Ferguson inherited the mill, then derelict, which was once worked by Robert's father. Now the big wheel rumbles and vibrates through the boards again as it grinds flour in the traditional way. There is also a fascinating costume and farming artefact display, helpfully labelled, which brings alive work on the land. The Ferguson family will probably be encountered in the wholesome coffee-room—real soup and irresistible cakes—and are infectiously enthusiastic about their project. Visit it because the display is thoughtful, informative and entertaining—many of Scotland's 'official' or

*Dalgarven Mill*

more highly funded museums could learn much from it. Best of all, the owners are local folk who have gone back to their roots.

Follow signs through Kilwinning for **IRVINE**. Here you will find the **Scottish Maritime Museum**. This somewhat spread out and still expanding collection has a quayside exhibition hall where the story of floating transport is told. There are also actual floating exhibits downstream and a shipyard worker's house. It is altogether a curious mix. If you have just come from Dalgarven Mill you may find the exhibition hall labelling and presentation a little too neat and impersonal.

On your way out of slightly uninspiring Irvine (though it has a massive leisure centre by the sea) look for the Ayr road—you can visit the **Heckling Shop**, a shop/museum with an audio-visual display in the restored Glasgow Vennel on your left at the south end of the town (Townhead). This is only one of the quite confusing range of places associated with Robert Burns, Scotland's national poet. (Burns worked for a time as a flax-dresser or heckler.) There is an official Burns Trail which reaches a positive frenzy at Ayr, your next destination down the coast. Take a dual carriageway section of A78/A77 from Irvine to this substantial seaside town, with the final approach by A719.

**AYR** pop. 50,000    Largest of the traditional Clyde coast resorts. Tourist Information Centre: 39 Sandgate (0292 284196). The town has extensive sands, a harbour, plenty of shops and most of all, a host of signs pointing out places associated with Robert Burns. Many of them are south of the town in the suburb of Alloway. However, from the busy town centre you can take a short walk to cross the River Ayr by one of 'The Brigs of Ayr'—the title of a Burns poem. The pedestrians-only, picturesque Auld Brig, restored in 1907, dates at least to the 15C; some historians say it is older. The New Bridge, which carries the A719, post-dates Burns. On the main street you will find the **Tam o' Shanter Museum**, an inn and brewhouse in Burns' time. The original Tam o' Shanter of Burns' famous poem was Douglas Graham of Shanter Farm. His adventures are described below. Between main street and river is the **Auld Kirk**, really the New Church of St John the Baptist, completed about 1654 following the building of a Cromwellian fort on the site of an earlier parish church. Many of Burns' contemporaries are buried within the churchyard. The walls of Cromwell's fort survive in the middle of a residential area nearer the beach.

To reach the other Burns venues leave Ayr on A719, looking for signs to the left, past Belleisle Park, which point to **Burns Cottage and Museum**. The poet's thatched and humble birthplace is now next-door to a leading Burnsiana museum. A little southwards is the **Land o' Burns Centre**, round the corner from which is the neo-classical **Burns Monument** in a garden overlooking the River Doon. Also here are the shell of **Alloway Auld Kirk** and the **Brig o' Doon**. Note the distance between these two places most particularly. This is the stretch galloped by Tam o' Shanter's grey mare Meg, bearing home a drunken Tam, after he had been unwise enough to call out encouragement to a novice witch. She was one of a gathering in the kirkyard, who was dancing in a short shirt or 'cutty sark'. Tam was spotted and pursued, and Meg lost her tail as horse and rider just made it across running water. All this is in the narrative poem 'Tam o' Shanter'—a dramatic tale of drunkenness and orgies amid what is now the respectable leafy suburb of Alloway: prescribed reading for all non-natives on this route. All Scots know it already!

Return to A719 and note in passing **Greenan Castle** by the shore, suggested by an American researcher as being the site of King Arthur's Camelot. The road then climbs by the Heads of Ayr on to the long flanks of the Carrick Hills sweeping down to the coast. It passes ruined **Dunure Castle** seen below on a side road. (The Earl of Cassilis once roasted the lay-abbot of Crossraguel here in a subtle attempt to persuade him to give up the abbey lands.)

Beyond, while apparently going downhill, look for a sign **Electric Brae**. Because of an optical illusion, the usual notions of uphill or down do not apply here. Take great care as there will probably be a few cars proving this for themselves by rolling backwards up the hill with total disregard for other traffic. The phenomenon is definitely not caused by electricity.

If your attention can divert from other vehicles erratically crawling up/down a hill, then look south for a view of **Culzean Castle** in its wooded grounds by the sea edge. Reach it by keeping to A719, which goes right, signed Maidens, then follow castle signs. This is the NTS's most popular property. The castle's wooded 'policies' became a country park with sheltered walks, ancient trees and dazzling rhododendrons, a notable herbaceous border in the walled garden and lochs with superior-looking swans. A reception and interpretation centre can be found in the former farm buildings which are now the base for the park's ranger-naturalist service. The castle itself, castellated, opulent and arrogant above the waves, was built round an ancient tower of the Kennedys and is considered one of Robert Adam's finest creations. Magnificent plaster work, the oval staircase and the round drawing room are just a few of its interior splendours. Make sure you find the informative panorama board in the immediate castle grounds looking west to Arran.

Back on the route, and as a down-to-earth alternative to NTS catering, you can enjoy a straightforward home-cooked pub lunch at the **Masons Arms** at Maybole, on the main street towards the south end and only a few minutes east of Culzean by A719/B7023. (On the other hand, if you arrive at this point late in the day, Culzean Castle itself has a tourist information centre, as has Girvan to the south, which can both help with accommodation. If you want to explore the area in style, then you could stay at the **Kildonan Hotel** (046582 360/292) at Barrhill south of Girvan, a 1920s country house designed by Sir Edwin Lutyens for his son-in-law, then a senior-ranking politician. This plush mansion in the woods is well-placed also for joining the South-West route on p. 36.)

B7023 east from Maybole is also the key to the wilder part of Ayrshire and touches the top section of Galloway. Look for the sign to Straiton. Go through **CROSSHILL**, neat white cottages in a green fold, and past Blairquhan Castle tucked out of sight in its grounds behind a high wall, to reach Straiton on B741. Watch for the sharp left in the village. Here the lushness and hawthorn hedges drop away as the road climbs into the high, thin sheep-pasture of the Carrick Hills, tattooed in places with conifer planting. At **DALMELLINGTON**, in a bowl of hills with grassed-over spoil-heaps and tips in a setting a little reminiscent of south Wales, the **Cathcartson Visitor Centre** in the middle of Dalmellington portrays the area's weaving heritage, though the venue is hard to spot. (Look for a white building right from the town-centre roundabout, near the burn.)

Continue on B741 to the main A76 at New Cumnock, where the difference between a rural setting and a scenic one can be appreciated. Go right, south-east, for **SANQUHAR**, home of the oldest post office in the UK (opened in 1763) as well as a fine tolbooth by William Adam (1735) and a local museum. Shortly after, beyond Mennock, turn sharp left on to B797 signed for Wanlockhead.

This adventurous road, the Mennock Pass, goes first into a steep-sided wooded valley, then up into the deep folds of high scree-flanked hills, finally to emerge amongst the open domed moors around **WANLOCK-HEAD**. This is the highest village in Scotland. At 1,400ft it is higher than any Highland settlement and the scenery on the climb up likewise stands comparison. It is also the home of the **Museum of the Scottish Lead Mining Industry**. The displays in the museum graphically tell the story of the mineral wealth of the Lowther Hills. Gold was first mined in the 16C and the area boasts a British mineral record of 70 different types. The lead mines reached their peak a century ago, closing in 1934. There is a beam engine and an optional underground excursion.

**LEADHILLS** is Wanlockhead's twin village, only a little further on— note on the left the trackbed of what was once the highest standard-gauge railway in Britain (1902–38). Enthusiasts are currently relaying part of the track in narrow-gauge. Leadhills also boasts one of the oldest public libraries in Britain, the **Allan Ramsay Library**, dating from 1741 and recalling the birthplace of the Scots poet.

Follow B797 which rolls down to Abington and the hurly-burly of the A74. Take this fast dual carriageway left for just a few moments, then exit on A73 for Lanark (also signed A702 Biggar.) Follow A73 round the flanks of Tinto Hill, noting the young Clyde on your right, to reach Lanark, the main market town of Clydesdale.

The history of **LANARK**, an early royal burgh, recalls the first of Scotland's freedom-fighters, William Wallace, who slew the English Sheriff of Clydesdale and committed the nation to rebellion. Few relics remain from these early times and most of today's visitors take the road down the hill to visit **NEW LANARK**.

With advice from the already successful English cotton mill pioneer, Richard Arkwright, the Glasgow entrepreneur David Dale chose New Lanark as the site for a major spinning development with labour organised in a totally new way. The first mill was opened in 1785 and soon a model village grew up around it. Dale, the well-to-do merchant and philan-thropic idealist, and, later, his son-in-law, Robert Owen, experimented with their vision of an ideal industrial community, self-sufficient with its own schools, recreation and decent housing. This was the birthplace of 'Owenism'—where exploitation of labour was balanced by the care and welfare of the workforce.

This community, cut off in the tree-filled gorge, diversified into other textile goods and experienced changes of ownership over the following century and a half, but much of the structure remained intact until the last works closed in 1967. Now this unique example of industrial heritage—houses, mills, shop and community facilities—has been saved. Suitably refurbished, New Lanark has applied for World Heritage Site status (like the Taj Mahal!). Visit today—it is best to park in the large car park and take the steps down the hill—and it becomes clear why Arkwright was so impressed with the site: nowhere else in Lowland Scotland does a great river roar through a narrow rocky channel with enough force to drive so many mills.

But there is another side to the community, away from the tall and austere blocks of houses. Walk through a gap in the wall at the far end of the site and you enter a world of woodland and mossy paths by a dark river. Walk upstream as far as the **Falls of Clyde**, firstly Dundaff Linn close to the mills, then Corra Linn, where white water spectacularly hurtles over carved sandstone, finally an impressive gorge section with views to Bonnington Linn. An autumn walk here is especially colourful. The Scottish Wildlife Trust care for this area and their information centre is in the village.

From Lanark take A72 towards Glasgow by the now gentler Clyde, past orchards which slope down to the river. Keep on this road until it crosses the M74, then turn right for Hamilton. Shortly after you will see signs for **Chatelherault** (pronounced Shatlerro.) On a slight rise stands a dog-kennel designed by William Adam! This venue is a reminder that the activities of the rich and powerful have always been a source of wonder and amusement to the ordinary folk of Scotland. The grassed-over parkland, dipping in places through mining settlement, was once the pleasure grounds of the Dukes of Hamilton around their seat, Hamilton Palace. This was the site in the 18C of one of Britain's most ambitious pieces of landscaping—involving a 3-mile-long avenue of trees, a fine lake and the Clyde canalised into order and harmony as a grand waterway.

Closing off the view was a dog kennel: a one-room deep façade with apartments, kitchens and staff quarters—and accommodation for dogs. This is the only building that survives today. The palace was demolished in 1927; the grounds had been mostly sold off for mining. The ornate façade of the dog kennel, reduced to a roofless shell, cost a breathtaking £7 million to restore in the 1980s as the focal point of what became a country park. An excellent visitor centre behind it tells the story of the estate by means of tableaux and displays. (Some of the realistic figures seem to escape disconcertingly into other parts of the centre. Look for the wife of the Fifth Duke, close by the cash-desk.) Certainly, Chatelherault gives food for thought, perhaps on the transient nature of such opulence. Return to Glasgow by the M74.

# The South-West

*2–4 days/230 miles (368km)/from Dumfries*

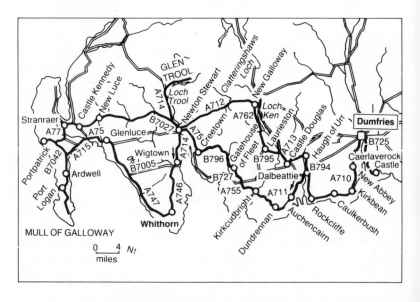

> *The Gallowaa Hills are covered wi broom*
> *Wi heather bells in bonny bloom*
> *Wi heather bells an rivers aa*
> *So we'll gang oot ower the hills tae Gallowaa.*

Traditional

Visitors from the south intent on pre-conceived ideas of Highland hills sometimes overshoot the south-west, the region of Scotland known as Dumfries and Galloway. This may be partly because the region on the Scottish Border is arguably the least appealing part of the entire area, welcoming the visitor to Gretna Green with a rash of tartanitis, usually caught in gift shops. One of the two venues associated with runaway marriages, performed until 1940, now advises that 'Amusing joke weddings are performed instead'. But persevere and turn left beyond the kilted haggises and whisky-filled mantelpiece scotty-dogs. Some miles west along the low fields of the Solway, the road to rural Galloway becomes more interesting.

The main road is the A75, carrying heavy traffic to and from the ferry ports for Ireland and the route described here avoids it wherever possible. Between the long sun-trapping shores of the Solway and the high moors to the north lies a network of minor roads encouraging detours. Agricultural traffic, sometimes four-legged on the way to the milking parlour, is a minor hazard to look out for—though you should find driving in the area very easy, because of the low volume of road-users on most roads. The south-west is a very easy-going, relaxed area. You can do this route in two days, but you should try to take much longer, as the area merits it.

**DUMFRIES** pop. 32,000  The region's largest town by far, and the real gateway to Galloway. As an administrative, commercial and shopping centre for a large hinterland it is inevitably busy and noisy, though the A75 bypass (open 1990) has improved the traffic-flow. Many of the older properties are built from Locharbriggs sandstone, the handsome local red rock. Even modern shop fronts in places harmoniously use the material, which adds to the town's reasonably pleasant shopping environment. Some of its main visitor attractions are linked with Robert Burns and include the major **Robert Burns Centre** with its displays and audio/visual presentations (and a good café). Other connections include **Burns House**, **Burns Mausoleum** and the **Globe Inn**, while the town's history is found in the **Dumfries Museum** and **Bridge House**. **Lincluden Collegiate Church**, just north of the town, is a 15C ruin on a site of early religious significance. Tourist Information Centre: Whitesands (0387 53862).

Near the town, to the south-east on B725, is the imposing ruin of **Caerlaverock Castle**, an unusual 13C triangular fortress. Also nearby is the **Caerlaverock National Nature Reserve**, an important area for wildfowl. This might be your introduction to the long shores of the Solway Firth. If standing with cold ears in an open salt-marsh is not your idea of birdwatching, then Caerlaverock should appeal. Well-placed hides and towers—some positively de luxe—ensure close views and comfort.

Cross the bridge over the River Nith to take A710 south from Dumfries. **NEW ABBEY** is only minutes away and offers a cluster of places of interest. These include the **Museum of Costume**, in Shambellie House amongst the woodlands—at time of last visit a slightly stiff and oppressive presentation—or, looming over the village itself, roofless **Sweetheart Abbey**, its worn stonework glowing red. A few moments walk away—but take care as the pavements are non-existent or narrow—you will find Historic Scotland's reconstructed **Corn Mill** (important: check the opening hours in advance).

Continuing along A710, the plantation-patterns on the slopes of Criffell on your right and the sands of Carse Bay on your left set the tone for the most typical of Solway scenes: moors above, sea below and all around lush green. Look for a sign at Kirkbean to **Arbigland**, a sheltered garden with stream-side primulas and other horticultural delights among protecting trees only moments from the coast. In the grounds is the cottage birthplace of Paul Jones, who founded the US navy and was in charge of several daring naval exploits around the British coasts in 1778.

The road then bears west, to Caulkerbush on the junction with the B793. If you go right here for about 2 miles (3km) you will find **Auchenskeoch Lodge** (038778 277). This small, friendly and very informal country house hotel makes an excellent base for exploring the area—though, with only five rooms, advance booking is wise. You should find that well-worn phrases like 'personal supervision of proprietors' and 'heart of the peaceful countryside' take on new life here. And don't be coy about accepting a second pudding—the other four tables already have! Ideally, you should explore the network of tiny roads all around, even on foot after the second pudding, the better to appreciate the woodlands and rolling, bright fields. (It is also only a few minutes drive to the coast. On the way, by a minor road south of Auchenskeoch Lodge, look for the kirkyard, near Upper Clifton Farm, with its interesting memorials, particularly a friendly little 17C skeleton carving!)

Also of note are the villas on the coast around **Sandyhills**, a reminder that the sands and low cliffs have for long been enjoyed as a resort area. When continuing your journey on A710 you soon reach the sign to **ROCKCLIFFE**, with well-kept little gardens carved out of the stonework, and home for all kinds of tender species. At the road-end you can take an easy path through scrub and open coastal woodlands, to **Kippford**, where neat bungalows doze gently in retirement. Return the same way, enjoying 'riviera' views of the blue shallows.

By now the A710 is immersed in rural Galloway. In spring there are sheets of bluebells spilling out from every shady copse, pink campion on the verges and bright yellow gorse. The main road loops up to **DALBEATTIE**, with silver granite to rival Aberdeen—and a similar tale of world-wide export from its local quarry. Though neat and attractive, the natural stonework of its sturdy cottages and civic buildings rather than painted frontages make Dalbeattie an atypical Galloway town.

Exit left from the top end of the town, cross a bridge beside the quarry and go left for Kirkcudbright on A711. The next loop is another relaxing drive, with trees and pasture giving a sense of stately parkland. The sea is glimpsed distantly, spilling into sandy bays on your left. On the coastal side, look for a sign to **Orchardton Tower** down a side road. This unoccupied 15C tower house is unique in Scotland because of its circular shape. At **AUCHENCAIRN**, birdwatchers or unhurried travellers may wish to digress left down the attractive shore road towards **Balcary Point**. Even non-birders should be able to tell an oystercatcher—black and white, orange bill—from a curlew—brown, long curved bill—as they

*Orchardton Tower*

hoover about in the sandflats only yards from the car.

Away from the coast, the hollow shell of **Dundrennan Abbey** soon appears out of the greenness. Here Mary Queen of Scots spent her last night in Scotland before exile. Beyond, it is a straightforward run to Kirkcudbright by the main road, though it passes by a variety of unsavoury warning notices. The military took over the area during the Second World War and still retain it.

To avoid this brief stretch, and as a very peaceful and short adventure, there are back roads which also take you westward to Kirkcudbright. Turn sharp right by the church in Dundrennan, before you reach the abbey. Go uphill by a narrow road, veering right at a grassy triangle, then left at a junction passing a cottage, Burnside, and a farm. Follow this road into Kirkcudbright, by way of the dip in which is the Buckland Burn, then another downhill section, turning briefly left on B727. The prevailing colour is the brightest of green, unless you also meet the farm collie which is blurred grey and may attempt to bite the tyres off at speed. This is ultra-rural Galloway.

**KIRKCUDBRIGHT** (pronounced 'kircoobree') is a cheerful and multicoloured little town, with a tidal riverfront and work-stained fishing boats. It has for long been associated with artists. The **Harbour Gallery** has changing exhibitions, while **Broughton House** offers a permanent display of the prominent locally born painter A.E. Hornel, only one of an increasingly fashionable group who worked here. Both places are close to **Maclellan's Castle**, a 16C castellated mansion, picturesquely ruined. Other attractions include the **Stewartry Museum**, pleasingly old-style in presentation and packed full of interest, and a large antiques warehouse notable in the town's good shopping selection.

Cross the bridge on A755, west of the town, heading for Gatehouse of Fleet. At a staggered crossroads on A75, go carefully left and right to join B727 for **GATEHOUSE OF FLEET**. A peaceful little pastel-painted place, Gatehouse's main link with the A75 is guarded by the foursquare **Cardoness Castle**, a typically severe 15C tower house. Follow the road through the village if you want to see it, noting the signs also for forest walks and viewpoints. Your route otherwise goes right at the Anwoth Hotel about halfway through, signed for Gatehouse Station. This is a particularly attractive section, which not only avoids the main road, but takes you, for the first time on this route, well away from the tang of the sea and up from the farms and lowland woods to the moors.

You climb by a twisting ferny-walled road from the tall trees of the valley of the Water of Fleet to an area of uplands in places torn for conifer planting, backed by dark hills and a distant but impressive railway viaduct. (This was part of the old 'Port Road', the main line from Dumfries to Stranraer, closed in 1965.) Beyond Gatehouse Station, which is just that and no more, follow the road left in a gentle burnside loop back down to the low ground at **CREETOWN**. Here you will find the **Gem Rock Museum**, an impressive collection of rocks and minerals of all kinds. One novel feature is the shelves of dull looking stones which are transformed under ultra-violet light into unearthly glowing shapes—in short, they fluoresce. There is also a gem-cutting workshop and a café and shop area; overall a most interesting experience.

From Creetown make your way right and right again to join a new stretch of A75 as far as **NEWTON STEWART**. This substantial town, with a good shopping choice and a local museum, is a natural route centre with touring options at every compass point.

These include a tour of the **Machars**, the rural, rolling lands to the south. Take A714 for **WIGTOWN**, another well-painted and neat community with a wide main street, its own local museum and a sad tale of the Covenanters. Two women were tied to a stake and drowned here for their faith in 1685. This is only one example of the religious fanaticism which blights Scotland's history in the 17C. There is a monument by the shore, or rather by the long flats of saltmarsh separating Wigtown from open water. South of the town is the **Bladnoch Distillery**, well away from the parts of Scotland usually associated with whisky distilling. It offers tours and a wee dram plus a reception centre and shop. You may find its single malt a particularly sweet, almost syrupy, but certainly smooth and mellow distillation.

In the Machars there is a sense of openness in the landscape and of wide breezy skies. About three-quarters of the land area is permanent grassland for dairying. The heavy soils hereabouts are made from the glacial material dumped and shaped into little whalebacks (drumlins) during the last Ice Age. These gorsy hummocks edged by 'dry-stane dykes' stand in green tides of pastures, with cows wading in immaculate black-and-white costumes. The Machars are also well known for pre-historic and early Christian sites. Most of Scotland's ancient places need a lot of imagination to reach back to the very dim past, and the cairns and tumbled rock-slabs hereabouts are no exception. In the area around Wigtown are such prominent examples as **Drumtroddan** with its standing stones and cup-and-ring marked rocks and the **Torhousekie Stone Circle**, particularly well preserved. An OS map will reveal lots more.

To find the Machars best known archaeological site, continue south on A714, then take A746 for **WHITHORN**. You may pick up signs for this development from Newton Stewart onwards, as the **Whithorn Dig** is a major programme of excavation and interpretation of the early-Christian history of Scotland. A well-equipped visitor centre now fronts the village main street. This sophisticated and fascinating presentation explains the significance of Whithorn and displays material recovered from the dig site, just yards away. Next to the visitor centre is a pend or alleyway which has for centuries given access to the priory beyond. The names of the famous personages who have used this way are painted on the inner wall, among them 'Queen Elizabeth I (II of England) 1955', thereby keeping alive an old controversy!

Whithorn, from the Old English 'hwit erne', white house, was one of the first places in Scotland to practise Christianity, as early as the 5C (certainly before the island of Iona which claims to be the 'cradle of Christianity'). The white house was the Candida Casa, the 5C stone church built by the British priest St Ninian. (He was a Briton because the Scots at the time were still living in Ireland.)

Today visitors can enjoy the interpretative displays and take 'pot luck' with whatever is being investigated on the nearby dig at the time. There is also a reconstruction of a Viking House, as this many-layered site also had a Viking occupation. (Strictly speaking, this is a Viking House mark II. The first was burned down. In consequence the Whithorn Trust made the first-ever known Viking House insurance claim.) Adjacent is the **Whithorn Museum** with its collection of early-Christian crosses, and the whole complex is overlooked by the shell of the 12C priory, its Romanesque details carved when the religious site was already 700 years old.

Thus the Machars are full of early historical sites to delay you—you may wish to continue south to view St Ninian's Chapel at Isle of Whithorn (which is confusingly not an island)—otherwise take A746 south to join A747. Go right and northwards back up the coast. The road runs along the platform of a raised beach, giving good coastal views. A good Machars base is the **Corsemalzie Hotel**, particularly popular with fishermen. The hotel is tucked deep in the woodlands where only the eerie yelp of love-lorn tawny owls disturbs the dense black of the otherwise silent Galloway nights. The hotel is signed from B7005, which runs east–west from just south of Wigtown to A747 north of Port William.

A747 joins the new stretches of A75 near Glenluce, with **Glenluce Abbey**, an attractive fragment of a settlement founded in the late 12C, a little way up the valley of the Water of Luce. To explore the far southwest, known as the **Rinns of Galloway**, join A716 and follow it as it curves southwards. There are two contrasting gardens which benefit from the mild southwesterlies. The first, signed from the A715, is **Ardwell House**, an informal and pleasing display—definitely a working garden—around a substantial Galloway mansion. The second is the major collection at **Logan Botanic Garden**, an outstation of the Royal Botanic Garden in Edinburgh. Here the prevailing mildness is appreciated by a multitude of exotic species, including tree-ferns and blowsy magnolias. The garden is signed off B7065. You can continue on this road via Port Logan, across the ever-lush grazings to reach the southernmost tip of Scotland at the **Mull of Galloway**, a winding road across a rocky neck of land, collared with wave-bitten cliffs. There is a car park and a lighthouse—and a lot of sea between you and the Isle of Man.

Rejoin A716, taking B7042 for **PORTPATRICK** in a green amphitheatre by the sea-edge. This was a former ferry-port for Ireland and has a little rocky harbour and rows of neat and sturdy houses clustered behind. This is the starting point of the official long-distance footpath, the Southern Upland Way, 212 miles (339km) of walking against the grain of the land all the way to Cockburnspath on the east. It is also the site of the rather unexpected **Little Wheels Museum**, a childhood dream come true, with models galore, trucks and trains of all sizes including working layouts, great fun even if it isn't raining.

Take A77 for the quite substantial town of **STRANRAER**, a ferry-port which is imbued with a faintly end-of-the-line, windswept air. Watch out for Irish coinage in your change here! A little way back east, off A75, are the delightful **Castle Kennedy Gardens**. To be accurate, there are two castles in the spacious grounds. Castle Kennedy is a gaunt shell, burned in 1716, which stands behind the large hut comprising ticket office and cafe. Lochinch Castle was built in 1864 and is the home (private) of the Earl and Countess of Stair. At the start of the visit you can purchase a map and guidebook, though the ticket-lady's dog will offer to show you round. (Do not take up this offer unless you constantly want to throw sticks.) The gardens, really grand-scale pleasure grounds, are cleverly landscaped, with long vistas up avenues, or across massed azaleas to artificial lochs. The earthworks and broad plan were laid out by the Second Earl of Stair after 1733. While ordinary gardeners are content with a wheelbarrow, as he was a field marshal he had the advantage of a troop of soldiers which he used for major landscaping. The overall effect is breathtaking when the exotic shrubs flower—a strange blend of geometry and well-tended wildness, curiously dream-like and unrelated to the countryside around.

Immediately after you exit from the gardens back on to A75, go left up a minor road. This is a more pleasant way of returning to Newton Stewart: an upland excursion where green river valleys drop back for moorland lark-song, dry-stone dykes and rough pasture. At New Luce on the Luce Water, cross the bridge, go right, then left (unsigned) immediately after the kirkyard. This section has a slightly remote feel to it, before the conifer plantations block the views of the blue hills of the interior. Go left at a road junction, past three lochs and join B7027 at Glassoch Bridge.

Turn right and follow B7027 south to its junction with A714. This is only a short way from Newton Stewart, right. However, if you go left, there is a further excursion to what some claim to be the most picturesque spot in all of the south-west. Head north along A714, beside the smooth and sluggish Water of Cree which separates the road from the attractive **Wood of Cree**, an RSPB reserve. All the while you skirt the distant bulk of hills beyond the woodlands. Look for a right turn just beyond where the road crosses the river and follow further signs all the way through the trees, past Glentrool village to **Loch Trool**.

The road ends, rather suddenly, in a car park. Not until you walk a few yards to the rocky, heathery knolls at one side can you appreciate the vista. If you already know of the Trossachs near Stirling as a kind of yard-stick for typically Scottish scenery, then Loch Trool looks more like the Trossachs than the Trossachs do. High hills, their tops shorn bare and granite-grey by glaciers, crags, green- and purple-flanked, birch trees ringing with birdsong, a dark loch winding westwards—all help confirm the claim that you can see all of Scotland's landforms in Galloway.

Just to complete the picture, Loch Trool has a suitably important historical association. A short way above the car park is **Bruce's Stone**, an incised boulder recording Robert the Bruce's first victory over the occupying English forces in 1307 and the start of the Bannockburn campaign. The walkers' route to the Merrick, the highest hill in southern Scotland, lying to the north, starts from the car park. If this sounds too ambitious, you should at least walk among the rocky knolls for a view of the whole length of the loch in its wild setting. Then retrace your route to Newton Stewart.

To return eastwards, as ever keeping off the A75, go left within the town to cross the River Cree on B7079. Go left at its junction with A712. This is known as the **Queen's Way** a reference to Mary Queen of Scots, only one of the many monarchs and lesser folk who passed this way on pilgrimage to the religious centre of Whithorn. To be accurate, they passed on a roughly parallel path, marked on OS maps as the Old Edinburgh Road, now interrupted by the dammed Clatteringshaws Loch. This is only one of the ways in which the landscape has been greatly altered. The tall forestry plantations have already been felled in places, though the Forestry Commission does emphasise the recreational role of the woodlands—hence campsites and fishing lochs are signed, as well as a wild goat park and a deer range.

Another point of interest to look out for on the drive is **Murray's Monument**, a tall column on a rocky knoll commemorating Alexander Murray (1775–1813) a local shepherd's son who became Professor of Oriental Languages at Edinburgh University. At Clatteringshaws Loch, the Forestry Commission has a local wildlife display, the **Galloway Deer Museum** and you can also walk from there to another **Bruce's Stone**, set amid swathes of conifers by the loch.

A712 goes on to New Galloway at the top of scenic Loch Ken. Turn right to take the attractive A762 by the lochside then inland through fine rolling wooded landscapes to Laurieston. Go left here to take the equally attractive B795, then turn right for **CASTLE DOUGLAS**.

This pleasant little town has a long main shopping street (including a choice of good home bakeries) as well as a loch with boating. Nearby to the south-west, signed off the old A75 (the town is bypassed), are **Threave Gardens**. Surrounding a baronial mansion, Threave offers continually renewed plantings as the NTS use it as a training ground for their gardening staff. Thus there is a wide range of rock, water and shrub features, as well as a walled garden, all in a mature setting of tall trees. **Threave Castle**, again signed from the garden, lies to the north-west.

You park in a farmyard and walk down to the reedy river-edge. This bleak tower, once home of the sociable-sounding Archibald the Grim, is set on an island on the River Dee. Ring a bell to summon the boatman from across the water.

To return to the Dalbeattie area, the most attractive route is the old military road off the old A75 at the north end of Castle Douglas. Turn right just before a garage and check you are on the correct road by looking for a farm called Ernespie. The minor road rolls over the brilliant green to Haugh of Urr where you join B794, right and right again, to take you south for Dalbeattie down the valley of the Urr Water.

About a mile below Haugh of Urr, watch the fields on the left closely as one of the farms here still keeps the characteristic belted Galloway cattle. This local breed has fallen out of farming fashion—even the local tourist board has dropped them from its logo. You can travel the length of Galloway, as I did on this route's reconnaissance, and see mostly field-to-field Friesians. The belted Galloway is beloved of soft-toy makers perhaps because a family party of the beasts, full scale and on the hoof, looks exactly like a range of soft-toys anyway. (You could try Blowplain Open Farm to the north near New Galloway if you do not see them anywhere else.)

Just below and on the opposite side of the road from where the cattle *should* be, a high and gorsy hump turns out to be the **Motte of Urr**, considered to be one of the finest 12C earthworks in Scotland and, as huge mounds go, impressive in scale. Beyond, the road continues in a pleasant river valley to Dalbeattie and a choice of routes eastwards.

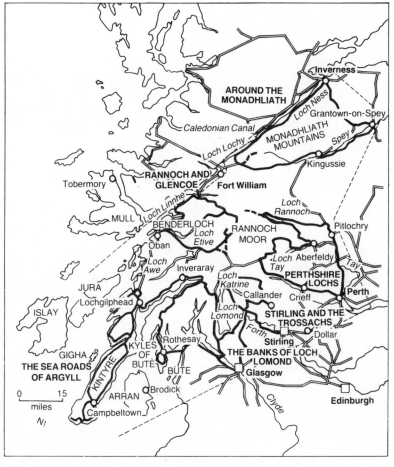

The southern edges of the Central Highlands are very easy to reach from the main population centres in Central Scotland. The Trossachs hills can be seen from Edinburgh Castle ramparts, Ben Lomond from high ground even to the south of Glasgow. The Highland Boundary Fault is an easily recognisable line. It starts, on the mainland, at Helensburgh on the Clyde estuary, runs through Loch Lomond and eastwards to the Trossachs, then on towards Perthshire and eventually into Angus.

Along the edge of the Highlands, little resorts sprang up, such as Callander, Aberfoyle or Dunkeld, catering for the tourist trade which began to gather pace from the early 19C. Though easily accessible, the hills and glens beyond certainly convey a sense of grandeur, with some of the most imposing mountain landscapes in Scotland to be found between the Highland edge and the Great Glen: Glen Coe, Glen Nevis or the hills of Perthshire are just a few examples from a magnificent choice.

# The Sea Roads of Argyll

*2–3 days/325 miles (520km)/from Glasgow*

> I had a particular pride in shewing him a great number of fine old trees, to compensate for the nakedness which had made such an impression on him on the eastern coast of Scotland.
>
> A Tour to the Hebrides
> Boswell, of Dr Johnson

If Glasgow is the gateway to the Trossachs to the north, then it is equally well placed for the west—the hills of Argyll and the islands in the great sea-way of the Clyde. The key to a speedy journey to this delightful area is the Clyde ferry services. Though Gourock to Dunoon is a possibility, this route takes you to Wemyss Bay and hence Bute. However, this little island is only the start of a tour which leads round and down to Kintyre via Knapdale with its fascinating early history. Do not make the mistake of assuming that Campbeltown, at the end of the long peninsula, is only a cluster of cottages. Instead it is a thriving town. On the way you can 'bag' Gigha and even return to Glasgow via the soaring granite of the island of Arran. This is a very flexible route easily expanded as the interest or weather dictates.

If you have to, you can hurtle out in little more than 40 minutes to **WEMYSS BAY** from Glasgow, past the shipyards, past Dumbarton Rock on the far bank, past the war-time convoy assembly points, in fact, past quite a lot of Scotland's decaying industrial heritage. Go left at a roundabout in Greenock, signed Largs—Wemyss Bay itself is a little reluctant to appear on signposts at first—and soon you arrive at Wemyss Bay and the large car park for the ferry. (You queue as there is no pre-booking for vehicles on this frequent service.) Once it was the native Glaswegian's delight to go 'doon the watter'—an excursion by steamer

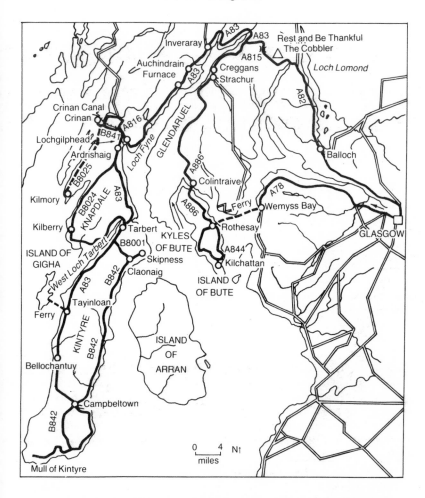

which was perhaps the only day's holiday the hard-worked ordinary folk would get from the 'workshop of the Empire'. Those days have long gone, though if you stroll into Wemyss Bay station next to the car park you will find intact the old Glasgow and South-Western Railway Company's magnificent wrought-ironwork which supports a curving canopy leading from platform to pier.

Once on board Caledonian-MacBrayne's Rothesay ferry and nearing the island of Bute, look to port for the almost palace-fronted symmetry of the Victorian mansions built along the south side of Rothesay Bay. These are just some of the fascinating echoes on Bute of the 'doon the watter' days. Some of **ROTHESAY**'s faded hotels still lean towards the clashing wallpaper, crusted ketchup and plastic flowers school of catering, though there is some good basic fish and chips to be found. Aside from its resort architecture the town's main places of interest are its unusual circular-walled castle once stormed by the Norse, its local museum, Ardencraig Gardens—though you may still find the slightly 'time-capsule' ambience the most fascinating aspect of the place.

Take the main promenade road southwards, A844, leaving sturdy Victoriana behind for a rocky shoreline with lounging eider ducks. Go left on a minor road in the trees, signed Kingarth via Bruchaig road. This gives bright green and beech-hedge views in a surprisingly gentle and rural landscape. The road swings west to give the first views of the Arran hills (which will rear up at regular intervals throughout this whole route) beyond the curve of sandy Kilchattan Bay. Rejoin the main road at Kingarth, continuing west for a short way to find a road, left, signed St Blane's Chapel. This little road rises over a ridge of volcanic basalt and soon gives outstanding views of the gaunt hills of Arran beyond Bute's shattered coastline. There are ancient hill forts in the vicinity, and evidence of later Norse occupation, as well as seashore caves once used by the distant Neolithic folk. The local tourist information centre will supply leaflets to help in the interpretation but if time is pressing, restrict your excursion to a short walk up to **St Blane's Chapel**. (There is a small car park beside a farm-sign reading 'Plan'.) Blane was a nephew of Cattan, fellow student of the famous Columba. Its setting amongst crags and tall trees has helped retain its unspoilt, peaceful air. It is a place for pausing and contemplation by the ancient mossy stones.

Retrace your route to the main A844 then drive north, enjoying the seascapes and sandy bays. On the way you will notice the north of the island is rougher and less cultivated. Keep on A844 by going left to pass Ardscalpsie Bay. At this point you cross the Highland Boundary Fault, which accounts for the landscape change. The comparatively fertile red sandstones of the lower third of the island are replaced by gritty rocks weathering to poor moorland soils which prevail to the north. You can follow A844 to its end beyond Ettrick Bay then take a long walk along a track for fine views of the Kyles of Bute. However, this route should have given you a flavour of the rural attractions of the island so far removed from Rothesay. Thus take B878 for Rothesay, at the promenade turning left and northwards along the coast for the ferry at Rhubodach, another frequent service which takes only five minutes to deliver you to the mainland at Colintraive.

The next section of the route, A886, gives glimpses of the eastern 'leg' of the inverted Y of the Kyles of Bute, then the base of the Y, shallow Loch Riddon. The road slices through rock to make a quick and easy passage through the wild scattering of birch and oakwoods which part-clothe rugged uplands, before dropping into flat-bottomed and buzzard-patrolled Glendaruel.

In turn the glen leads over the watershed and opens into views of the long fjord of Loch Fyne. Continue on the main road, heading north-east to join A815 at Strachur, going left. Moments later this brings you to the **Creggans Inn** (0369 86279) which has a very friendly bar and offers informal bar lunches. (NB: Given an early start from Glasgow, it is perfectly possible to see Bute and reach this point for lunch.) Standards of accommodation and evening meals here are also very high, though not inexpensive.

Beyond Strachur, the road continues by Loch Fyne, with rhododendron thickets choking the woods in places and the mossed-over narrow old road glimpsed in the fields nearby as a reminder that travelling here was not always so speedy. A815 then climbs to a road junction with A83 amongst the high green hill slopes. Go left then down towards Loch Fyne, passing **Strone House Gardens** in the trees below you, left. On its shady woodland walks with their exotic shrubs, you can also see what is claimed to be Britain's tallest tree, a Grand Fir in excess of 200ft (61m). A83 rounds the head of Loch Fyne and turns, at last, south. Note the **Loch Fyne Oyster Bar** with its appetising array of fresh seafood both in its shop and its pine-clad all-day opening restaurant.

The approaches to **INVERARAY** are notable for some fine bridgework. The first is the Garron Bridge 1747–9, designed by Roger Morris and built by John Adam, which has a slightly Chinese 'willow pattern' look about it. The next is the bridge over the River Aray, Robert Mylne, 1773–6. These are just a foretaste of the extraordinary architecture of the town itself. Inveraray is no piecemeal Highland hamlet but an ordered settlement and outstanding example of 18C town planning instigated by the Third Duke of Argyll. Some of the finest contemporary architects were involved in the grouping of buildings; the neat, white symmetry of the town seems hardly removed from a drawing board idea of the enthusiastic Duke. **Inveraray Jail** has been restored and is now a visitor attraction with set-piece courtroom and prison scenes with lifelike figures. Even the smells are authentic! Also in the compact little town is an attractive granite bell tower with one of Scotland's finest peals.

The nearby seat of the Campbell Dukes of Argyll is at **Inveraray Castle**, a mansion started in 1743 (like the town) with subsequent alterations and involvement of the Adam family of architects. You will notice this stately pile in grey-green stone on the approaches to the town. There are historical relics and portraits on view and nearby is the **Combined Operations Museum**—a reminder that this little settlement in the sleepy hills was once a military training centre for some of the major actions of the Second World War, including the Normandy Landings.

Continue south-east on the main road, which temporarily leaves the loch-side for the forested hills and soon reaches **Auchindrain Museum**. This has been created from an 18C communal tenancy farm. Many farm buildings have been restored and furnished in period and there is an interesting interpretation centre and shop.

A83 then returns to the loch at Furnace, the name recalling 18C ironsmelting using charcoal from local woodlands. This industry has now vanished, like the Loch Fyne herring which once played an important part in Scotland's fishing industry. The road goes on to reach **Crarae Glen Garden** where the climate of Argyll demonstrates what mild and moist means in gardening terms. Beside Crarae Lodge, a burn flows steeply downhill in thick woodlands which have been likened to a

*Auchindrain Museum*

Himalayan valley. Certainly, as you stroll below paddle-leaved rhododendrons dropping red trumpets on the ground, with magnolias and other exotica shining out of the greenery, the ambience is almost too lush to be Scottish. Continue on A83, which eventually swings round the bite of Loch Gilp, a small Loch Fyne offshoot. The views all the way across the salt waters to the hills of Cowal are pleasant without being over-grand.

The local centre of **LOCH-GILPHEAD** is a pleasant and neatly painted Argyll town, with a wide and sometimes bustling main street and a good selection of shops. Here A83 meets A816, the long artery running down from Oban to the Mull of Kintyre. Both the area south of Lochgilphead, known as **Knapdale**, and a stretch to the north are noted for early historic sites.

Another place of interest nearby is the Crinan Canal. To take in these points, join A816, going right (signed Oban) just west of Lochgilphead. Continue north with the levels of Crinan Moss stretching west of the River Add. Look for a sign to Dunadd, about 4 miles (6km) from Lochgilphead, where a track goes left. Go down it to a signed car park. Today **Dunadd Fort** is a breezy and rocky hump rising from the low land. Yet in the 6C it was established as the centre or capital of the kingdom of Dalriada, founded by the Scots who came (whisper it) from Ireland. No buildings survive, though there is a basin, a footprint and an evocative outline of a boar cut into the rock.

Return to the main road, going left, then left again off it to reach a crossroads. Go left on the long straight of B8025 to reach the **Crinan Canal**. This waterway was authorised as early as 1793, partly to assist fishing vessels and allow them access to Hebridean grounds without rounding the Mull of Kintyre. It was eventually opened in 1801 but needed much subsequent renewal in which the distinguished engineer Thomas Telford was involved. Cross the canal and turn right for **CRINAN**. About a mile further, as the canal turns north, go left then right to follow the road past the front of the Crinan Hotel—which looks like the bridge of an ocean liner—to find a large car park. There is an appetising coffee shop here, much frequented by yachting types. The little harbour where the canal 'locks down' to the open sea is hemmed in by a bowl of steep tree-clad slopes. Space seems at a premium, both ashore and afloat.

Then return along the canal banks all the way to the B841/A816 road junction. [There is another option here: take B8025, going south, just east of Crinan, then go left along the east shore of Loch Sween on a minor road. Your rewards will include some lonely white beaches, sculptured gravestones at Kilmory, outstanding views of Jura and also the oldest stone castle on mainland Scotland, the mid-12C Castle Sween, on the sea-edge unhappily close to a caravan park. Please note that you cannot take your car round in a full circle, though some maps show otherwise. You must return to Crinan.]

At the B841/A816 junction, go right and south, bypassing Lochgilphead, and continuing past Ardrishaig, the other end of the canal. Take B8024, signed Kilberry. This road gives good views back to the Cowal Hills before breaking across moors then dropping into woodlands by Loch Caolisport. The next stretch is delightful, with spring primroses, mossy walls and honeysuckle tying down the wind-carved woods. The promise of ever-improving island views across a glittering sea is fulfilled as the road climbs away from the raised beaches of the rocky shore. The Paps of Jura and the less distinguished hills of Islay fill the western horizon, with yellow gorse as the perfect photo foreground.

There are more ancient carved grave slabs at **Kilberry**, housed in a permanent stone shelter and perhaps less distinguished than either Kilmory or Kilmartin. Just beyond them, back on your route, is the **Kilberry Inn**, with a good reputation for informal food. A little further, the Arran Hills on the skyline beyond Loch Stornoway are a reminder that you now are looping north to reach West Loch Tarbert, again in a pleasantly wooded landscape, eventually to return to the main road by a signed minor road short-cutting the head of the loch. Go right and south, signed Campbeltown, noting the ferry-pier for Islay, a little way down.

The next section of A83 leads speedily into Kintyre, gradually exchanging a Highland flavour for wild seascapes. The powerful landowning Campbells settled the peninsula with Lowland farmers and the western margins have a green fertility reminiscent of Ayrshire. This is particularly noticeable on the stretches of the road lower on the peninsula which take advantage of the prominent raised beaches. Left of the road are stranded cliffs, complete with old 'sea-caves in places, while on the right are the flats of green fields stretching to the shore. At little settlements such as Muasdale, dark and detached rocks rear up out of fields and gardens, as though the tide had just gone out to reveal grass and houses instead of rockpools.

With mountainous Jura slipping back to the north, lower-profiled Islay stretches along the horizon with the smaller dark and low-lying shape of **Gigha** lining up in front of it. This attractive little island is reached via a 20-minute ferry-crossing from Tayinloan. Its main attraction is **Achamore House Gardens**. It is feasible to leave your car at Tayinloan, take a morning ferry across, walk (20 minutes) from ferry pier to the gardens and return to the mainland in time for a late lunch. The gardens, sheltered by tall trees, feature many exotic species as well as lichen-encrusted azaleas and positive thickets of camellias. Make sure you discover the viewpoint beyond the walled garden, from where you can appreciate just how narrow Gigha is, with an almost simultaneous view west to Islay and east to Kintyre.

A good base for this excursion, as well as the exploration of the rest of the Kintyre peninsula, is the **Putechan Lodge Hotel** (05832 266/323) at

Bellochantuy. Set below the stranded cliffs by the shore, it is so much a part of the rocky environs that sea-pink (thrift) seeds itself happily on the patio. This former shooting lodge of the Dukes of Argyll has been thoughtfully upgraded and extended by its owners over the years. Comfortable and spacious, it offers quality cuisine in a genuinely friendly ambience. It is one of the very few Scottish hotels which is silent enough for you to appreciate a gentle morning call from oystercatchers piping on the rocky shore.

Continuing south, soon the main road reluctantly gives up its fast run along the coast—though not before allowing the briefest glimpse of the long crescent of yellow sand which stretches to Machrihanish. Then rolling green fields lead on to the major Kintyre centre of **CAMP-BELTOWN**. Creameries process the milk from the local dairy herds, while local whisky distilling still survives. With its Woolworths and its local shops, its own newspaper office, fishing boats by the pier, Campbel-town has the flavour of a Lowland community.

The **Mull of Kintyre**, famed in song, is a further 10 miles (16km) down the peninsula, reached by first taking the Machrihanish road, then follow-ing signs for Southend, where the beach is overlooked by **Dunaverty Rock**, a former castle site with a bloody history in the Covenanting wars. Also by the shore, on a rocky mound, are the imprints of what tradition calls **Columba's Footsteps**. You can see these before looping on to the narrow road which leads across rough rolling ground to the lighthouse at the Mull. Park before the road goes down the steep hill which falls to the sea—the lighthouse itself is surprisingly low down—and the best views of Ireland can be had from the adjacent moorland. Try to be there for sunset, as the coastline at this point looks due west. Retrace your route to Campbeltown—though you might alternatively take the little coastal road that loops by the eastern shore from Southend back to the main town.

To contrast the two coasts of Kintyre, return northwards on B842, which starts along the north shore of Campbeltown Loch from the town. This road is narrow and winding in places and care is needed, but the views of the Arran Hills across Kilbrannan Sound are reward enough. As well as wild seascapes there are wooded stream valleys with narrow stone-parapet bridges. The bare remains of **Saddell Abbey** are signed, and this once-prosperous 12C Cistercian House has a varied collection of carved gravestones. Beyond Carradale the road develops a more Highland flavour and runs briefly inland, with looming well-clad hills to the west, then it returns shoreward with Arran at its closest. At Claonaig the summer-only ferry runs to Arran (p. 99) enabling you to island-hop to Ayrshire.

Alternatively, by going right at Claonaig and continuing past the ferry pier, you come upon the extensive high-walled remains of **Skipness Castle**, the earliest parts of which date from the 13C. It was once an important seat of the Lords of the Isles. Then return to Claonaig and drive over the moors to drop back to the main A83, turning right to make the easy journey back to the head of Loch Fyne via West Loch Tarbert, Lochgilphead and Inveraray. From the top portion of the loch, the fastest way to Glasgow is to stay on A83 which leads into the dark rocks of Glen Kinglas, climbs the watershed by the alpine-flavoured uplands to the **Rest and Be Thankful** before hurtling down Glen Croe amongst the trees of the Argyll Forest Park. The profile of **The Cobbler** is the most easily recognised peak among the dark screes. Beyond Arrochar and the naval paraphernalia on Loch Long, join A82 at Tarbet on Loch Lomond, returning to the Lowlands at Balloch.

## The Banks of Loch Lomond

*1 day/108 miles (173km)/from Glasgow*

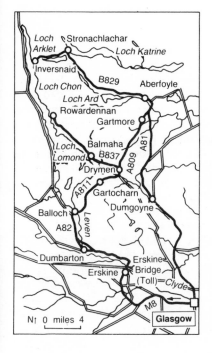

*O let them be left, wildness and wet;*
*Long live the weeds and the wilder-*
*ness yet.*

'Inversnaid'
Gerard Manley Hopkins

The spruced-up image and new confidence of Glasgow is beguiling enough to merit leisurely exploration. But if you finally tire of outstanding Victorian architecture, the biggest range of shopping in Scotland, outstanding museums and art galleries and all its other plus-points, then take advantage of another of Glasgow's attributes: its nearness to the Highlands. For generations, the 'Bonnie, Bonnie Banks of Loch Lomond' (written by a Jacobite prisoner in Carlisle) has sentimentally tugged at the Scottish heart-strings. True, Loch Lomond has a special place, and is a byword for fine scenery. However, it has gained this reputation partly because it is the nearest chunk of attractive countryside to the Clydeside conurbation and acts as a great green (and purple) lung, a whiff of Highland air and long-established outdoors escape route. It also happens to have the largest surface area of any loch in Scotland at 27.45sq. miles (71sq. km), though Loch Ness is bigger in volume and Loch Morar deeper.

The easiest way out of **GLASGOW** (see p. 30) is the westbound M8/A8, leaving this busy route to cross the Erskine Bridge (toll 30p) which is

*Dumbarton Rock*

well signed. This joins A82 for **DUMBARTON**, built round the landmark of Dumbarton Rock. This former work-stained industrial centre, currently dusting itself down and tidying up, is interesting enough if you enjoy industrial heritage—for example, you can view the unique **Denny Ship Model Experiment Tank** which, as its name suggests, is a large tank with appropriate apparatus formerly used for testing the design of ships' hulls in model form. Some of the most famous Clyde-built liners were designed here. Dumbarton is really Dun-Briton, the 'fort of the Britons' and the still-fortified rock marked the centre of this early tribe's Strathclyde kingdom.

Press on, following A82 signs as the road sweeps north into the industrialised Vale of Leven. The whisky warehouses and grey housing blocks of Renton and Alexandria are built on material dumped by a glacier. **Loch Lomond** is dammed (glacially speaking) behind this, only 27ft (83m) above sea-level with the River Leven as its sea-connection. You may lose heart hereabouts, as the tentacles of undistinguished built-up areas stretch nearly all the way to the loch shore.

Yet you are still only 30 minutes from the city centre. Go right (east) at the roundabout to A811. **BALLOCH**, of no particular distinction, still intrudes, though you can get closer to the loch at **Balloch Country Park**, signed left. Better, however, to shake off the last of the housing, reaching pleasant, gently rolling farming country on the 4 miles (6km) to **GARTOCHARN**. Behind the village you will notice a little plum-pudding. This is Duncryne Hill. Park and climb it—go right—for one of the finest views anywhere in Scotland. This should only take a few minutes. As you look out, you will see that the loch, released by the pincers of the Highland hills to the north, spreads wide in the foreground, lapping the Lowland greenery and lush hedgerows. The nearest islands run in a line which marks the Highland Boundary Fault: soft red sandstone underlies the immediate area, over which the Lomond glacier once spread. North, the great hills are made of resistant schists and other tough rocks; Ben Lomond is one of the tallest in the ranks of high hills between which the loch twists. Altogether a dramatic, living geology lesson! There are leafy, wild-rose lanes to explore nearer the loch, if time permits.

Otherwise, continue eastwards, beyond the twisting Endrick Water as it seeps into wildlife-rich marshlands. Then follow signs to **DRYMEN** by the A809/B858. Drymen is discreet and neatly clipped, with slightly unexpected fashion shops as a reminder that these country, tweedy places close to the city are rather well-heeled. Try the **Salmon Leap Inn** (0360 60357), cheerfully serving good food. Turn left in Drymen for B837 to Rowardennan.

After 3 miles (5km) of fields and mixed woodlands, you meet the loch shores at **BALMAHA**, a 'cottagey' kind of community below tall larches, with a large car park to indicate its day-visitor popularity. From here, boat cruises go round the islands—**Inchcailloch** with its unspoilt oakwoods is highly recommended. The West Highland Way, one of Scotland's sign-posted 'official'—and hence grossly over-used—long-distance footpaths joins the road here, down from the humps of Conic Hill.

All the way to **ROWARDENNAN**, about 7 miles (11km) above Balmaha, the road, though narrow, is a delight. Bird-song rings out from the oak wood's canopy, in contrast to the dim, dark green silence in the pine plantations. The loch, seldom more than a field's length away, glitters through the alder-clumps. There are tempting picnic sites and forest walks. At Rowardennan the road stops, with a large car park, toilets and information boards. The site is a study in leisure: high-fashions from swinging Glasgow trip over earnest hillwalkers stooping to lace up their boots. The main path for Ben Lomond, one of Scotland's most popular 'Munros' (collective name for peaks over 3,000ft/914m in height), starts from here. If more gentle exercise is also on your programme, simply follow West Highland Way signs north, along a forestry track through sheltered woodlands.

In any case, you must return to Drymen to continue your drive, taking the unclassified, single-track road due north out of the village (past a pub called the Clachan). This route traverses higher ground than the parallel main road to Aberfoyle. The back road gives glimpses, to the left, of Loch Lomond and the serpentine back of Conic Hill, marking the geological change from Lowland to Highland, the Highland Boundary Fault. Eastwards the wooded flats of the upper Forth Valley can also be seen. Beyond the white houses of Gartmore in a sylvan setting, this back road rejoins the main A81 for Aberfoyle.

Continue straight through Aberfoyle to B829, the second cul-de-sac road on this excursion. It is likewise through high-grade scenery, with views across **Loch Ard** (particularly its east end) which may send you skidding suddenly into laybys and fumbling for the camera: reeds, misty water, pine-spiked moors, cloud-topped mountain—the perfect picture postcard!

Beyond Loch Ard is gloomy **Loch Chon**, which has a grim old legend about a dog-headed monster partial to passers-by. Keep camera at the ready, not for fabled beasts, but for a later view. Beyond the loch, the road soon climbs out on open moorland and the western horizon opens up. **Loch Arklet**, in still conditions, will mirror the peaks known as the Arrochar Alps. They seem to rise behind the loch, but Loch Arklet is separated from these mountains by the glacial trough of Loch Lomond, deep cut and out of sight.

B829, close to the old rallying place of Clan Gregor, meets an unclassi-fied road at a lonely T-junction. As you should visit both ends of this little road, choose right or left in either order. Left, in 3 miles (5km), takes you past the shores of Loch Arklet and the old garrison above **INVER-SNAID**. A farm name recalls the site of this garrison built to house troops sent in by an irritated government, determined to curb the unruly Macgregors. The road drops into tangled woodland and emerges at Inversnaid on Loch Lomond—little more than a large hotel and an even larger car park, yet a spot much more peaceful when contrasted with the fierce rush of traffic noticeable on the far side of the loch.

Here again you meet the West Highland Way. The path north, up the lochside, is reasonably dry at this point and is recommended for a stroll, unless being overtaken by dedicated long-distance walkers makes you feel guilty. This is also the site of the waterfall with its 'Wiry heathpacks, flitches of fern, and the beadbonny ash that sits over the burn' which inspired the English poet Gerard Manley Hopkins' 'Inversnaid'.

Retrace your route, zigzagging up the hill and go on at the road junction for barely a mile to **STRONACHLACHAR** (practise pronouncing the Scots 'ch' sounds in private first). This is no more than a few neat houses. Strathclyde Water Board will not permit you to take your car any further than the neatly hedged car park, but walkers and cyclists can use its well-maintained roads which run most of the way round Loch Katrine, Glasgow's water supply. One road leads eastwards only as far as the sluices at Royal Cottage, while the other goes first west to Glen Gyle, once an old cattle droving route, before doubling back east to connect with the public road system at the main Trossachs car park. Glen Gyle, just out of sight up the loch from the car park, was the birthplace of the most famous of the Clan Gregor: Rob Roy Macgregor, part rogue, part Gaelic Robin Hood.

At Stronachlachar, looking across the loch to empty hill-passes, in the past regularly used by a now-vanished population, there is a strong sense of the Highlands of old—and a sharp contrast to the bustle of the Lowlands, to which you should now back-track. Return to Aberfoyle and follow A81 from the village this time, aiming for the hump of Dumgoyne, the last flourish of the Campsie Hills before they drop into Strath Blane. The rock-terraced end of the uplands here is a last reminder of the wild places before the urban paraphernalia of Glasgow, Scotland's largest city, is reached.

## Stirling and the Trossachs

*1 day/80 miles (128km)/from Stirling*

> High in the south huge Ben Venue,
> Down on the lake in masses threw,
> Crags, knolls, and mounds, confusedly hurled,
> The fragments of an earlier world.

'The Lady of the Lake'
Sir Walter Scott

In 1794 the local minister of Callander wrote in a published description of his parish: 'The Trossachs are often visited by persons of taste, who are

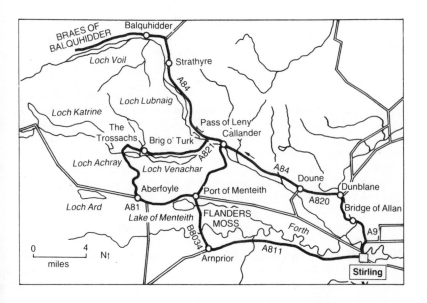

desirous of seeing nature in her rudest and most unpolished state'. By the early 19C, the growing cult of the picturesque and the Romantic movement had made the Trossachs a favourite location for sightseeing, even before Sir Walter Scott peopled the lochs and dark woods with knights, hermits and fair ladies. Like Loch Lomond to the west, these landscapes on the edge of the Highlands had the advantage of relatively easy access from the populated Lowlands. This excursion follows in the footsteps of those early tasteful travellers, starting from the Central Highlands gateway of Stirling.

**STIRLING** pop. 30,000   Tourist Information Centre: 41 Dumbarton Road (0786 75019). In former times the lowest bridging point of the River Forth. The Gargunnock Hills below, the Ochils above, marshes to the west and a wide river to the east meant that all roads led to Stirling and it developed as a strategic centre with a fortified rock. The marshes today have been turned into fertile fields, the river is no longer a barrier, but the hills remain and the fortified rock is still topped by the impressive **Stirling Castle**. For long the favourite residence of the Stuart monarchs, it still boasts some of the earliest French Renaissance architecture in Scotland, though the fabric was treated shamefully by the military who used it as a barracks after the Scottish Court removed to London following the Union of the Crowns. There is much to see, both within the castle walls and in the old town immediately below it, where there are some fine restored buildings around Broad Street. The tolbooth and mercat cross are a reminder of commercial life in an old Scots burgh. Stirling, in essence, gets newer as you travel downhill. **Darnley's Coffee House** in Bow Street at the bottom end of Broad Street offers a home-baked respite if you are exploring the old town area on foot. Yet further down the hill are the Victorian shopping streets and a modern shopping arcade, the Thistle Centre, making Stirling one of the most interesting towns from a town planning viewpoint, with each succeeding wave of building clearly marked.

Another way of discovering Stirling's key role in Scotland's history is to visit the NTS's **Bannockburn Heritage Centre**, east of the town. In 1314 Robert the Bruce chose the field carefully for Scotland's greatest victory—one of the very few—over the English. The terrain, low and marshy running down to the Forth, was ideal for bogging-down the heavy horses of the armoured English knights. Not choosing it for scenic appeal, it is not his fault that it has subsequently become a nondescript housing scheme. An audio/visual display helps to bring the past alive and there are other Scottish figures to meet, including a rather unexpected Mary Queen of Scots, playing tennis in alarming pantaloons.

Near **Old Stirling Bridge** (possibly late 15C, pedestrians only) follow A9 for Bridge of Allan. You can navigate by the conspicuous column of the **Wallace Monument**. If you visit this Victorian shrine to another of Scotland's freedom fighters, the ascent to the top of the monument up a tight spiral stairway gives a breathtaking view, though you may have little breath left in any case after the dizzying climb. There are also audio/visual shows here, with the voiceovers sounding their reverent incantations over Scotland's heroes or Wallace's sword, and strangely echoing in the cold stone halls. However, the tea-room is friendly.

*The Wallace Monument*

**BRIDGE OF ALLAN** is a former spa town. Its **Royal Hotel** (0786 832234) serves a competent pub lunch. Continue to the round-about at the top of the M9, taking A9, right, for **DUNBLANE**. This attractive little community is built around its much restored **Cathedral**, mainly 13C, in a peaceful square, with bustling shopping streets nearby. A820 westwards leads on to Doune, though the parallel B824, a mile to the south, gives finer hill views. **DOUNE** was once a centre of pistol making. **Doune Castle** is one of the best preserved medieval castles in Scotland and stands on an imposing river-side site.

Join A84, turning right for Callander and passing the **Doune**

**Motor Museum** on the way, which features the world's second-oldest Rolls-Royce. Ben Ledi lures you on and then seems to loom from the end of Callander's main street (particularly if you use a telephoto lens). **CALLANDER** is a long-established place of resort for Sunday trippers from the Lowlands, overnight tourists on their way to the west and longer-stay visitors exploring the woods and crags of the Trossachs. Callander's shops seem ever open and its streets bustle with strollers all day. **Dalgair House** (0877 30283), an inconspicuous frontage on the main street, offers friendly and flexible meals in a pleasant and well-polished ambience, though the **Roman Camp Hotel** (0877 30003) down by the river is even more peaceful. This 17C former hunting lodge of the Dukes of Perth is a welcoming, wood-panelled haven from the busy town, though only moments from the main street. Its cuisine is outstanding.

Many visitors are too intent on window-shopping to discover the impressive **Bracklinn Falls**, a short but rewarding walk from a good car park in the woodlands above the town, signposted right, before you reach the centre. The more energetic can enjoy further woodland walks taking them high on **Callander Crags** with superb views over the treetops and town, down to the Lowlands as far as the Pentland Hills. The **Rob Roy and Trossachs Visitor Centre** acts as a gateway and starting point for visitors heading due west.

The Trossachs excursion normally is taken in a loop by turning left beyond Callander. But first, for a further flavour of hill scenery, continue on A84. Pause at the **Falls of Leny** overhung by oak and fir, then continue to **Loch Lubnaig** and **Strathyre**. The first real Highland glen, by **Balquhidder**, is on the left. This cul-de-sac unclassified road westwards goes as far as the flanks of high Stob Binnein and Ben More, passing Loch Voil. There are good picnic spots. In the landscape, sheep farming, new tree planting and the scars of forestry access roads have all made their mark—an easily reached tableau of the Highlands, attractive in spite of all. **Rob Roy's Grave** is often visited in Balquhidder churchyard. This cattle-dealer, rogue and folk-hero was a staunch Jacobite who outwitted the government armies in the troubled times of the uprisings and eventually died peacefully at home in Balquhidder in 1734.

Retrace your route back to the Trossachs junction, as the views of the woods and crags above Loch Lubnaig are just as good in the reverse direction. Take A821 westwards. **Loch Venachar** is the first and gentlest of the Trossachs lochs, beyond which lies **Brig o' Turk** where the woodlands begin to close in. Turk is 'tuirc', Gaelic for wild boar, alas, long extinct. There is a good pub and restaurant here, hospitable and well run, **Dundarroch and the Byre** (08776 200).

**Loch Achray**, only yards beyond, is more typically 'Trossachy', a suitable preliminary for the signpost that leads down a short bendy road by mossy crags and birches. This narrow pass leading to **Loch Katrine** is the very heart of the Trossachs. Confirmation of its status comes with the size of the car park by the narrow, twisted end of Katrine. Everyone is here—tour buses, strollers, hikers, dogs and bairns. Yet walk along the

*Loch Katrine and SS* Sir Walter Scott

private road (Strathclyde Water Board), that continues along the lochside for a mile or two and you will leave most of them behind. The Trossachs has a strange capacity to mop up visitors and lose them in the landscape. Part of the reason for the popularity of this spot may come from the *Sir Walter Scott*, a 90-year-old steam-powered cruising vessel, which operates in the summer season.

Return to the main A821 and let it take you gently into the higher moorlands. Much of the area was planted before the Second World War by the Forestry Commission and thus tall trees hem in the views. Ben Venue and Ben Ledi ride over an endless rolling pine-green sea as the road snakes round knolls and heathery hummocks. Look for Loch Drunkie, glinting distantly amongst the dark trees to your left. Soon, but not before allowing the views over the Highland edge to be seen from the **Queen Elizabeth Forest Park Centre** (the former David Marshall Lodge), the road zig-zags down to **ABERFOYLE**. Go left at the road junction. There is not, in truth, a great deal of interest down here, apart from its scattering of souvenir shops, though the huge car park on its former station site may lead you to think otherwise. However, the **Scottish Wool Centre** will definitely improve the visitor options.

Take A81 out of the town, now heading east. This soon passes the **Lake of Menteith**. This is really the 'laich' (of Menteith), a Scots word meaning low-lying ground, but this early map-maker's misunderstanding is now fixed in the tourist-brochure description as 'Scotland's only lake'.

Mary Queen of Scots was taken to the lake/loch here in 1547 and rowed across to **Inchmahome Priory**, its island setting a place of safety for her in her troubled homeland. There is a little ferry connection in the summer months to this ruined 13C Augustinian house. The rough conglomerate rock of the knobbly Menteith Hills immediately to the north marks the Highland Boundary Fault.

The return route to Stirling takes in some fascinating geological features, formed where Highland and Lowland meet. Take B8034 on the right, southwards. The Lake of Menteith is a giant 'kettle-hole' formed by the melting of a huge ice-block, while this pleasant country road through mixed woods and pastures crosses the humps and hollows of material dumped by a glacier a mere 10,000 years ago.

Turn left at Arnprior on to A811 (signed for **Kippen**, an old established community on higher ground with views across the carse—a convenient Scots word for a river plain). Between Kippen and the Trossachs hills lie well-worked flat fields, stitched together by hedgerows. These were once the great marshes and bogs of which Flanders Moss, the partly tree-covered uncultivated stretch below Kippen, still remains. The rest, once the Ice-Age estuary of the River Forth, afterwards a peat-covered wilderness, was drained from the 18C onwards. A811 hugs the edge of the carse, passing close to Gargunnock, another pre-drainage settlement on higher ground, and returns to Stirling, showing the castle in photogenic profile.

# Perthshire Lochs

*1–2 days/165 miles (264km)/from Perth*

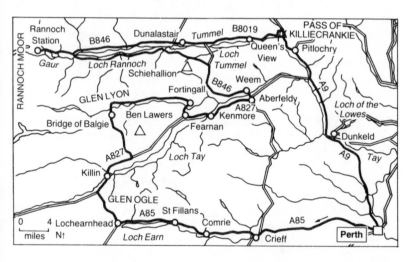

*The mist rose and died away, and showed us that country lying as waste as the sea; only the moorfowl and peewees crying upon it, and far over to the east, a herd of deer, moving like dots.*

Rannoch Moor
from *Kidnapped*, Robert Louis Stevenson

Perthshire is sometimes called 'Scotland's Hampshire', for reasons which may be to do with its sense of discreet rural cosiness behind high walls. Or it may be a reference to the sights on Perth's shopping streets at weekends when the county set, all camouflage headsquares and four-wheel drive wellingtons, sally in for their shopping. But there is a wilder aspect to this old county which styles itself 'heart of Scotland': high green hills, fragments of the ancient Caledonian forest and winds singing through empty moorland wastes—the landscapes of Robert Louis Stevenson's *Kidnapped*.

**PERTH** pop. 42,000   Tourist Information Centre: The Round House, Marshall Place (0738 38353). A busy, go-ahead town on the Tay (now bypassed by the A9), with an easy-to-follow grid of shopping streets as well as a history which stretches back to Roman times. Near it is the ancient capital of **Scone**, while within the town are historic venues such as the **Kirk of St John's**. Here John Knox preached a sermon against idolatry which sent a destructive mob raging through the town and ultimately through all of Scotland. The **Fair Maid's House**, recalling Scott's heroine in the 'Fair Maid of Perth' is another of the town's oldest buildings, now housing a changing crafts and art exhibition. **Balhousie Castle**, in which is the Black Watch Regimental Museum, the **Art Gallery and Museum**, with local history and whisky industry displays, and the **Bells Sports Centre** are other diversions within the town, as are visits to crystal glass and whisky bottling plants. As for upmarket shopping, as well as a wide range of tweedy fashions and delicatessens, you can also inspect the largest pearl ever to be found in a Scottish river. Literally 'beyond price', it sits on display, glowing pinkly in the gently opulent premises of **Cairncross**, jewellers and goldsmiths, in St John Street. (The pearl has been named 'Little Willie' after its finder.) Finally, **Branklyn Garden**, on A85 eastwards, is a charming and secluded planting, small enough to inspire the modest gardener.

Take A85 west from the town, noting the twin joined keeps of **Huntingtower** gradually losing the battle with encroaching suburban sprawl. Further out, well-kept woods and plantations, prize beef cattle, rustic gate lodges and tidy farms are a reminder that the Highlands do not yet dominate. Even at **CRIEFF**, a genteel town built on a tilt, the high hills seem to recede ever-further westwards.

*Crieff*

Most visitors, chequebooks at the ready, head downhill to the Earn riverbank and the **Crieff Visitor Centre** with its blobby paperweights and thistle-bedecked pottery. Opposite is a crystal glass-making company. However, a stroll up **Knock Hill** (watch for red squirrels), above the town, involves no risk to your holiday budget. There are fine views across to the Ochils, with Strathearn rolling out between. Nearby is the **Glenturret Distillery**, reached by a signed road beyond the town, on the right. Tucked into a high glen, Glenturret offers an insight into distilling by way of friendly tours and a well-equipped heritage centre. You can also have lunch in its restaurant.

Beyond Crieff, the countryside takes on a more Highland aspect. At **COMRIE**, Scotland's earthquake centre from its position on the now-familiar Highland Boundary Fault, you will find the **Scottish Tartans Museum**, a serious collection of over 450 tartans and other materials relating to Highland dress. The Highland backdrop begins to close in thereafter, with heathery crags leading on to **St Fillans** and **Loch Earn**. A85 here takes the north bank. Note also there is a minor road along the south bank—slower, narrower and therefore more peaceful.

More than half-way along the loch, the great scree-face of **Ben Vorlich** rears out of its glen to the south, on your left. The settlement of **LOCHEARNHEAD** is strung along the western end of Loch Earn. It has a water-sport centre and tends to cater for the boisterous dinghy and water-skiing fraternity. At the junction with A84, go right and into **Glen Ogle**. The gradient up this impressive glen was shared with the old Caledonian Railway's line to Oban via Dunblane and Callander, until a rockfall finished it off in 1965, ahead of its scheduled closure. It was said that the end-on view down Loch Earn as the track wound round a high hill shoulder was the finest from a railway carriage anywhere in Britain.

On 10 September 1842, Queen Victoria, travelling down the glen, noted of the scenery that it 'puts one in mind of the prints of the Khyber Pass'. She too had no doubt enjoyed the views eastwards of the Ben Lawers range, from the top of the pass. At A827 on the other side, turn right for Killin.

**KILLIN** has a little of the flavour of an alpine village, especially when the snows lie late in spring on the tumbled ridges of Meall nan Tarmachan high above. When passing through the village, most folk stop in the car park beyond, then return to peer over the narrow bridge at the **Falls of Dochart**, foaming their way down to the great Loch Tay beyond. Fewer seek out the ruins of **Finlarig Castle**, complete with beheading pit. On a lighter note, you can enjoy a straightforward, wholesome meal at the popular **Shutters Restaurant** (05672 314) on the main street.

From Killin a minor road goes east along the south shore of **Loch Tay**, but continue on the main A827. The gentle slopes to the lochside are well-farmed on the northern side, though there are ruined and deserted settlements as a reminder of a once larger population. About 5 miles (8km) east of Killin look for a minor road, left, signed for **Ben Lawers** and Glen Lyon. If you are an early spring visitor this way may still be blocked by snow. Check for warning notices.

This narrow little road heads steeply up and out of the valley with superb open views of the rich green slopes of the Ben Lawers range. The 'base-rich' (i.e. alkaline) rock hereabouts contrasts with the more typically poor and acid Highland moorlands. Because of its relative fertility, the area contains a rich relic arctic-alpine flora on the rocky heights of Ben Lawers (3,984ft/1,235m). It is of great botanical importance and therefore worthy of protection. The NTS's efforts to this end involved plonking a **visitor centre**, a bizarre and brutal intrusion, amongst the high grasslands. Consequently, Ben Lawers, botanical treasures notwithstanding, is one of the most often visited of Scotland's peaks, with all the attendant problems of path erosion and disturbance.

The little road levels off, beyond the centre, passes Lochan na Lairig, dammed as part of a hydro-electric complex, and loops round heather-covered knolls giving northern mountain views. Then it gently drops into beautiful **Glen Lyon** at Bridge of Balgie. With its typically glacial U-shaped profile, steep hills on either side, winding river and mixed woods, Glen Lyon has high-grade scenery throughout its length.

Here turn right, though if time permits the upper glen, to the west (left), shows other typically Central Highland features worth exploring. These include a private castle amongst the riverside trees, high side glens or 'hanging valleys' and at the head of the glen, a 1,740ft-long (540m) dam which doubled the size of Loch Lyon. (The road which some maps show going south from Loch Lyon to Glen Lochay is private.) But for all the landscape and loch tinkering, Glen Lyon still has an unspoilt air, with superb views of the long shoulders of the Ben Lawers complex southwards, and peaks almost as high to the north, above woods and steep heathery slopes.

You may easily pass shattered heaps of stones by the river flats without realising that these are the remains of stone towers associated with the Irish hero, Fin MacCool. Glen Lyon, in legend, was once his home: 'Twelve castles Fionn had, In the Crooked Glen of Stones.' The legends came from Ireland, as did the Scots who imported them and ultimately defeated the Picts. Glen Lyon is a shadowy place, where grassed-over mounds and rocks have ancient names.

Following the route down the glen, past rocky falls and wooded narrows, you reach **FORTINGALL**. This is a pleasant hamlet with some unusual (for Scotland) thatched houses. It is also known for the **Fortingall Yew**. This 3,000-year-old tree, split, gnarled and with its limbs resting on the ground, is thought to be perhaps the oldest living tree in Europe. It is linked with a delightfully improbable local tale that Fortingall was the birthplace of Pontius Pilate. His father was a Roman centurion stationed here—or so the story goes ...

From Fortingall go south at the Bridge of Lyon for Fearnan on Loch Tay-side. You will find a good choice of accommodation in the Fearnan/Kenmore/Aberfeldy area. Turn right for neat little **KENMORE**, at the head of Loch Tay, where you can stay at Scotland's oldest inn, the **Kenmore Hotel** (08873 205). The area around Loch Tay and beyond to the west was once entirely Campbell country. In 1903, after 500 years of ruthless acquisition by the family, the Marquis of Breadalbane held almost half a million acres. No wonder a satirical poem was printed at the time in *Punch* 'From Kenmore to Benmore/The land is a' the Markiss's'. By 1948 all of it was gone, fulfilling a well-documented 17C prophecy of a local seer, the 'Lady of Lawers'. Taymouth Castle was once the family seat. Now its grounds are a golf course. (While in Kenmore, note in passing the

*General Wade's Bridge, Aberfeldy*

spectacular road zig-zagging south-east up and out of the village. It gives outstanding views of Schiehallion from the top before dropping into lonely Glen Quaich to reach the A822 Crieff to Aberfeldy road through the Sma' Glen, hence returning east to Perth.)

Take A827 from Kenmore to reach **ABERFELDY**, a pleasant little community dozing on the river-flats of the Tay. Within the town you should take tea at **Country Fare** (0887 20729) in the main street—home-bakes and whole-some soups, everything impeccably clean. (You should pause here because, if time is short, you may want to omit the next loop, and head east instead to the A9.) To reach Rannoch, go back westwards along the north bank of the Tay on B846, which follows the old military road over to Rannoch and crosses **General Wade's Bridge** of 1733. Though amongst the finest of Wade's Highland bridges, the elegant and pleasing lines indicate that it was in fact designed by William Adam. (For more information on military roads, see the Loch Ness route, p. 73.)

Still close to Aberfeldy, beyond Weem with its steep woods, is **Castle Menzies**, a good example of a Z-plan 16C fortified tower house. It is in process of restoration by Clan Menzies, whose museum it houses. B846 soon leaves the open valley and climbs northwards, passing close to Fortingall. Continue uphill.

The rock-dappled flanks of **Schiehallion** become prominent as you climb up to the Rannoch water-shed. By the road is the **Glengoulandie Deer Farm** with its red deer, 'Heilan coos' and some rarer species. At almost the highest point on this stretch a minor road cuts across Schiehallion's shapely shoulder. Go left here. The Astronomer Royal in 1777 chose Schiehallion's slopes for his experiments to determine the weight of the earth. (This involved, in part, measuring the deflection of a pendulum by the mountain's proximity.)

The route rolls down from the high silvery quartzite screes to the flat valley floor at **KINLOCH RANNOCH**, where there are shops and hotels. **Loch Rannoch** stretches west with roads on both banks. Take the south side, unclassified, road for views of the loch through a pine edging. The steep valley slopes are forested on your left. Some of this tree-cover is a surviving chunk of the ancient Caledonian Forest which once covered much of the Highlands. Unlike the prickly dim dankness of a modern plantation, the best and natural parts of the **Black Wood of Rannoch**, in spite of its name, are light and open, studded with great-limbed Scots pines and with an understorey of juniper and high heather. Look for crossbills, especially the exotic brick-red males, just one of the wildlife specialities of this fascinating area. There are several picnic sites and signed trails.

At the west end of the loch, the road crosses the River Gaur to join B846. Since you have come this far, you may wish to go all the way to **Rannoch Station** a further 5 miles (8km), in which case go left. There is no through-route across the **Moor of Rannoch**, except for walkers. As you approach the wild wastes of Rannoch, by way of a twisty road across the hummocky heather lands and a tumbling river, you can muse on the thought that this furrowed desert of peat was once a great reservoir of ice. The glaciers rumbled out in all directions from this centre, carving the loch-channels seen on this drive, as well as some mentioned in other routes. Look at the map of Scotland and note the pattern of Lochs Etive, Awe, Fyne, Lomond, Katrine, Earn, Tay, Rannoch and others, broadly running out like the spokes of a wheel. They all point towards this great depression, seen from the road-end at Rannoch Station.

The one hotel here takes some advantage of the lack of competition. For a full flavour of the moor, cross the West Highland line and stroll by **Loch Laidon**, with a plantation as a windbreak on the north side. The hills of the Black Mount mark the western borders of the emptiness. Ahead, in the *Kidnapped* adventure, somewhere in the peat-hags and black pools, David Balfour started from sleep to find a troop of redcoats bearing down on him and fellow-fugitive Alan Breck Stewart. Their line of escape was northwards towards still-remote Ben Alder.

Return on B846, past the little power stations and weirs on the River Gaur (and the unseen feeder tunnels which form part of this huge hydro-electric network), then along the north side of Loch Rannoch where Schiehallion presents its most dramatic steep-coned profile amongst the birches. Continue from Kinloch Rannoch, past Dunalastair Water, taking B8019 by the shores of Loch Tummel, going steadily eastwards for a last look back at the woods and hills from the **Queen's View** as the road climbs high above the lochside.

Queen Victoria enjoyed this view in 1866, though there was probably not a car park and café then. She also missed the **Tummel Forest Centre** where today's visitors can learn about the work of the forester.

The quickest return to Perth is by the hurly-burly of the greatly improved A9. However, there is a good range of attractions, for example between Killiecrankie and Perth, sometimes missed by single-minded tourers whizzing north or south. Take a minor road north from B8019, just before the A9 junction. This leads on to the **Pass of Killiecrankie**, with two-fold interest: firstly as a place of great beauty with forest walks through natural oak-woods, tall, ancient larches and impressive river scenery; secondly, for the National Trust for Scotland's visitor centre which tells the story of the Battle of Killiecrankie. This was the first of the Jacobite uprisings in 1688. The Jacobite forces won the day, but as their leader, Graham of Claverhouse, 'Bonnie Dundee', was killed, they were unable to press home their advantage.

Turn south for **PITLOCHRY**. This long-established resort in the hills offers craft and souvenir shopping in abundance, as well as a wide choice of pubs and tea-rooms. It also offers interest at the **Faskally Dam Visitor Centre**. Its exhibition makes sense of the great Tay catchment area which you have just explored. The nearby fish ladder enables salmon to bypass the dam and, incidentally, to swim past a glass panel in order to study the visitors. Pitlochry features the **Pitlochry Festival Theatre**, running an easily digested summer programme from its 'theatre in the hills'. It has a café/restaurant with wholesome food and long opening hours. You can also go whisky-tasting near the town at the **Edradour Distillery**, which claims to be the smallest in Scotland.

Continuing south, rejoin A9, then leave it again for **DUNKELD**, crossing the Tay by Thomas Telford's bridge of 1809 to reach this cathedral community. The NTS has been at work here restoring domestic properties under its 'Little Houses' scheme. The pleasing results can be seen in the main square (opposite the excellent fish and chip shop, much appreciated by southbound hungry skiers in winter!). The houses were all built after 1689 because the Jacobite victors of Killecrankie came south, attacked Dunkeld and were fended off by the Cameronians, though the town was gutted by fire. There is more military history in the local **Scottish Horse Museum**, which recalls the yeomanry regiment founded by the Duke of Atholl. **Dunkeld Cathedral** nearby was wrecked at the Reformation and partly restored. Much of the remains are 14C and 15C. The choir is roofed and serves as the Parish Church. Off the main street, by the river, there is a large antiques shop which makes an interesting browse.

Finally, within easy reach are the **Hermitage**, an 18C folly set above the wooded gorge of the River Braan (signed westwards from the A9), and, east of Dunkeld, off A923, the Scottish Wildlife Trust's visitor facility at **Loch of the Lowes**, which features ospreys in season, so to speak.

Return to Perth on the A9, which loses its Highland flavour immediately south of Dunkeld.

# Rannoch and Glen Coe

*1 day/90 miles (144km) (basic circuit)/from Oban*

*Mists and storms brood over it through the greater part of the finest summer; and even on those rare days when the sun is bright, and when there is no cloud in the sky, the impression made by the landscape is sad and awful.*

Lord Macaulay on Glen Coe

Oban is given as the start of this loop only because it is the largest centre in the area—many other places on the way offer accommodation. This circuit takes in some of Argyll's finest mountain scenery—notwithstand-

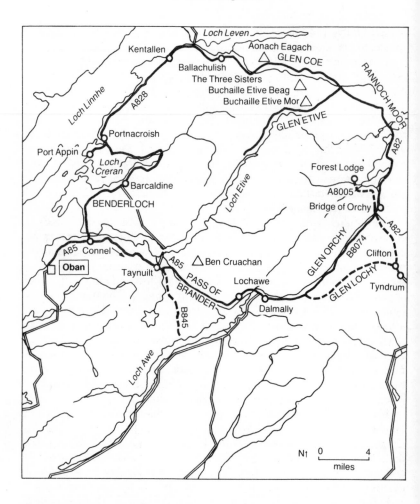

ing Macaulay's gloomy view—as well as a flavour of the Great Glen, an ancient fault line which wrenched the top half of Scotland sideways and south-west for 65 miles (104km)—geologists have matched up rocks to north and south of the glen to prove this!

**OBAN** is an old-established west coast resort, which has been festooned with B&B signs for generations. Rail-head and island gateway, little wonder it is a hectic place in high season (or at least as hectic as anywhere in the West Highlands can be). With tartans and ceilidhs breaking out throughout the town, Oban single-mindedly sets out to service its visitors with entertainment, a large choice of accommodation, much of it in solid Victorian guest houses and hotels, as well as restaurants, pubs, a breezy seafront and all the tempting permutations of island visits or cruises.

If you have chosen Oban as your base, make your way north-east on A85.

About 2 miles (3km) out, **Dunstaffnage Castle**, the headland stronghold of the MacDougalls, still commands the sea-lanes of this nautical cross-roads by the Sound of Mull and the Firth of Lorn. Further on, at Connel, your landmark is the sturdy bridge designed for the Caledonian Railway by the son of Isambard Kingdom Brunel. Below the structure, when the tides are right, the **Falls of Lora** foam fearsomely in the narrows. With the salt-water shores of the long Loch Etive on your left and the end cone of Ben Cruachan ahead, continue on A85 to **TAYNUILT**. Here, the **Bonawe Iron Furnace** does not cast an industrial pall on the landscape, as it is the preserved remains of a 17C furnace, which produced charcoal for iron-smelting. The oakwoods of the west were formerly widely pillaged for this industry.

[At Taynuilt, note B845 on your right, heading south. This has fine surviving woodlands (RSPB reserve) and eventually leads to a minor road down the full length of Loch Awe. Off B845 is **Ardanaiseig House** (08663 333) whose gardens offer superb views back to the whole 'horseshoe' of the Cruachan range. Country-house-style food and accommodation here is also of the very highest quality.]

The main A85 now enters the narrow Pass of Brander and Loch Awe gradually opens out. Ben Cruachan is so close that its tops vanish behind a broad hillslope. High on the hill is a great dam, unseen from the main road, from which water runs down into Loch Awe and powers turbines on the way. The story of this 'pumped storage' scheme is told at the **Cruachan Dam Visitor Centre**. This offers minibus trips half a mile *into* the mountain. It is an ideal excursion for a wet day—and may be the only place in the Highlands free from midges.

Shortly after noting the restored Edwardian *Lady Rowena* steam launch offering cruises from the station pier at Lochawe, your eye will be drawn by a gaunt, turreted ruin on the grassy flats at the loch's eastern end. **Kilchurn Castle** was built in the 15C by Sir Colin Campbell of Glenorchy. It was once the powerbase of the Breadalbane Campbells and extensively rebuilt towards the end of the 17C. A century later it was all but abandoned as the Earls of Breadalbane developed Taymouth Castle instead. Visit this starkly picturesque and extensive ruin by parking beside the railway at the head of the loch, crossing the line carefully, then walking the prepared track across the (sometimes wet) fields. Panorama boards on the battlements help pinpoint the landmark hills all around.

With the hammerhead of Loch Awe butting against the dragon-back of Ben Cruachan and its high neighbours beyond, this is an area in which to savour the grandeur. Another excellent viewpoint can be reached via Dalmally. Go off the main road, right, and into the village following signs on to the old Inveraray road. This is open for motor traffic as far as the great granite stone monument to the Gaelic poet Duncan Ban Macintyre (1724–1812), the 'Burns of the Highlands'. Take plenty of camera film for the views from this brackeny knoll of the glittering loch, its islands and the mountainous backdrop.

Returning to the main A85, a little east of Dalmally, B8074 goes left and into **Glen Orchy**. This once well-populated glen was cleared in the early 19C by the all-powerful Breadalbanes. To this day there are still very few inhabitants. Look for the impressive waterfalls towards the east end, on a river which flows otherwise undisturbed—except for fishermen—through the woods of the glen (with good picnic spots).

[This route is an option contrasting with the main road which runs past Ben Lui and on via A82, right, to **TYNDRUM**, where visitor developments increase year on year. There are premises called, at time of writing, 'The Green Welly Shop', which neatly summarises this junction settlement, now even busier since the West Highland Way long-distance footpath arrived. Tyndrum also has an efficient refuelling stop, the **Clifton Coffeehouse**, offering a wide range of wares from home-bakes to history books. If you go to Tyndrum, make sure you backtrack west a few hundred yards on A82, then bear north and up the watershed to head for Rannoch.]

The Glen Orchy direct route misses Tyndrum and rejoins the main road before Bridge of Orchy. Today's A82 was built across the **Moor of Rannoch** in the 1930s. The old road, running to the west, nearer the hills of the Black Mount, is still passable for walkers. Motorists can use it as far as Victoria Bridge, a popular starting point for a wide choice of hillwalks for the fit and well-equipped. It is well worth taking this single-track cul-de-sac (A8005—less than 4 miles/6km long) for its fragments of old forest and outstanding hill scenery. Look for the signs from Bridge of Orchy, going left.

Otherwise you will find yourself motoring steadily downhill to the shores of Loch Tulla. Note how the West Highland Railway swings north-east for the roadless wastes of Rannoch, eventually to sneak into Fort William round the north side of the Ben Nevis and Mamores mountain barrier. The railway builders conquered the moor's wet sections by 'floating' the track, using masses of brushwood, pile after pile, to consolidate the track-bed.

Beyond the bridge at the end of Loch Tulla, round a sharp, climbing left-hand bend and after the road bears right again, look for 'the lone rowan tree', a well-known landmark. It grows from a crack in a great rock, on the left, safe not only from fire, but from the herds of nibbling sheep and deer which prevent much natural woodland regeneration throughout the Highlands.

A82 turns west at last, across a shattered mirror of lochs and gives the first glimpses of the portals of **Glen Coe**. All of this road section is well-engineered and speeds tend to increase here—perhaps it is the sense of excitement! The Great Herdsman of Etive, Buchaille Etive Mor, beyond the ski developments, draws the eye. On the right, **Kings House Hotel** (08556 259)—its name a reminder that this was once a hostelry on a military road—offers unflappable hospitality.

Beyond it, on the left, in the shadow of the rocky ramparts of the Buchaille Etive Mor, is the cul-de-sac into **Glen Etive**. This narrow road runs for about 10 miles (16km) to reach the shores of Loch Etive, the fjord-like ribbon of sea drawn far into the great hills (you left it at Taynuilt, near Oban). There are no roads down its banks and nor should you find in Glen Etive any hot-dog stalls or souvenir shops, or any other concessions to visitors except peerless rocky riverscapes and soaring, empty granite slopes.

On the main road into Glen Coe, admire the frowning buttresses of the Three Sisters to the left and the shattered pinnacles of the Aonach Eagach ridge, high on your right. (The Aonach Eagach is the mainland's most spectacular and airy ridgewalk and not for the faint-hearted.) Full information on the geology, pathways and history of this area can be found at the NTS's **Glen Coe Visitor Centre**; the Trust looks after the glen.

The story of the massacre in the glen in February 1692 of the Mac-Donalds by the Campbells is well known. Though the killings were bad enough, the deep sense of outrage felt in the Highlands, which still broods over these dark rocks today, stemmed from the revulsion felt for, not just murder, but 'murder under trust'. In a way difficult for modern society to understand—difficult enough for Lowland authorities even then—it was the usual practice in the Highlands to give food and shelter even to bitter clan enemies, should this be asked. This was just one example of the many ways in which moral and ethical codes in the Highlands differed from the Lowlands.

The MacDonalds, cattle thieves and raiders (in order to survive) and supporters of the exiled Catholic King James to boot, were among many troublesome clans. Their chief was late in swearing an oath to King William, giving the authorities the opportunity of making an example of them. Militia of the Clan Campbell (historically adept at turning up on the right side) marched on Glen Coe and asked for quarters. As a chief's hospitality was inviolable, this was gladly given. Acting on orders from the highest source, several days later these soldiers tried to wipe out the entire MacDonald settlement. The attempt was bungled, though more than forty men, women and children were butchered. Others escaped into the winter snow and died on the open hill. It was from this trust betrayed that the sense of outrage sprang.

The salt waters of the west are reached again beyond Glen Coe. Grey slate quarries were once worked at Ballachulish, but they have gone, along with the branch railway. Join A828 by the Ballachulish Bridge. A flavour of old railway days has been captured at the **Holly Tree** (063174 292) at Kentallen on Loch Linnhe's shore. The old station here has been revitalised and converted into a fresh and relaxed hotel and restaurant. The dining room extends over the old platforms, giving outstanding sunset views over the hills of Ardgour across the sealoch. The cuisine is imaginative and the owners cheerfully dedicated (and Scottish!).

A828 follows the shoreline southwards into Appin. The hills across the widening sealoch are on the other side of the Great Glen Fault line, which runs all the way north-east to Inverness and beyond (see the Great Glen route, p. 72). As you top a little rise, your eye will suddenly be caught by the romantic setting of **Castle Stalker** on its rocky islet, further

*Sea Life Centre, Barcaldine*

enhanced by the grey heights beyond the waves. Though the castle is private, it must be one of the most-photographed in the West Highlands. Choose your own angle—but take care how you park!

If time is not pressing, there may be a better view from the little road, right, beyond Portnacroish, signed for **Port Appin**. If you take this road, continue to the car park for the Lismore ferry, then walk a little way by a track down the coast to see a stranded arch. This strange hole in the cliff was cut by wave action in glacial times. The land all around here lifted as the glaciers melted, stranding the old shorelines. On the way there are good views of the green and fertile island of Lismore, the 'great garden' of Appin.

Continue on A828 round the head of Loch Creran, halfway down which is the **Sea Life Centre** at Barcaldine. Interesting and educational (in the best possible sense) for all ages, the centre gives more than a glimpse of the marine life around these shores and reveals that it is just as exotic as on any tropical reef. Some of the display tanks are of extra-ordinary shape and size: you can actually stand underneath a circling shoal of herring, for example or observe, nose-to-nose, a yard-wide skate as it rears up from the water to observe the onlooker. The wide range of facilities here includes a tea-room and shop.

A828 makes its way through the area known as Benderloch, returning to the coast to reach Connel via the old Ballachulish branch line viaduct, now taken over completely by the all-conquering motor car. Return to Oban by turning west on to the A85.

## Around the Monadhliath—The Great Glen and Speyside

*1 or (better) 2 days/140 miles (224km)/from Inverness*

*It was a delightful day, Lochness, and the road upon the side of it, shaded with birch trees, and the hills above it, pleased us very much. The scene was as sequestered and agreeably wild as could be desired . . .*

A Tour to the Hebrides with Dr Johnson
James Boswell

The Monadhliath (Gaelic 'Grey Moors') are the roadless rolling mountains south of Inverness. Their emptiness separates the cheery clutter of tourist Speyside from the Great Glen's monster mysteries. They form a rounded backdrop, on your left, throughout this trip, their domed

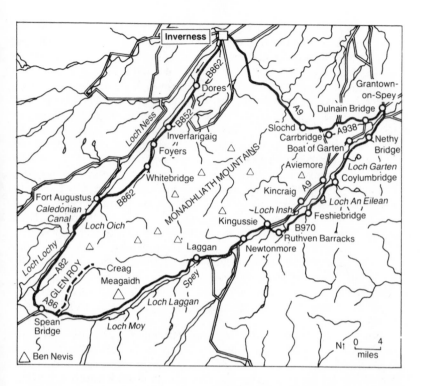

outlines gentler than the great gashed plateau of the Cairngorms on the other side of Strathspey. For the first half of this excursion, as far as the Spean Bridge turning, you roughly follow a 'Wade's Road', that is, the route of a military road built in the 1730s by General Wade's army squads in order that troops could move quickly, as the far-off London authorities were still anticipating trouble from Highland Jacobites.

**INVERNESS** pop. 40,000    Often called the 'Capital of the Highlands', Inverness is certainly not a remote clachan (hamlet) but a bustling centre with predatory traffic funnelling through one-way streets and where every requirement can be found, from Highland souvenirs to books and maps, plus all the 'High Street' stores to be seen in any other British town. Even though it can be bypassed by way of the Kessock Bridge, everyone, or so it seems in season, ends up here. There are open tailgates in every parking-space, as visitors anxiously over-stock for their future expeditions northwards. The town has few surviving early buildings because its strategic position on the edge of the Highlands ensured it was burned by wild clansmen at regular intervals.

Inverness is the gateway for **Loch Ness**. To avoid the fast and busy west bank A82, do not cross the River Ness but head upstream by its east bank, via B862 then B852. Loch Ness comes into view over the fields just before the village of Dores. For the credulous, monster spotting can begin here, especially in still, warm, mirage conditions, which the beast in the past has preferred. (The history of the phenomenon is told in the **Official Loch Ness Monster Exhibition** at Drumnadrochit on the west bank.)

The road continues along the lochside. It is narrow in places and gives intermittent views down the Great Glen through partly screening trees. There is a **Forest Centre** (Forestry Commission) at Inverfarigaig, with displays and a choice of forest walks. (If you look over the parapet of the nearby main road bridge, you will see the crumbling remains of a Wade's bridge in the greenery below.) The route then continues to Foyers, scene of the first commercial application of hydro-electricity (in 1896). As the road climbs away from the loch, look for the sign (opposite the shop) for the **Falls of Foyers**—though take care with children here as the paths which overlook a rocky black-water ravine are steep and slippery.

The road climbs and twists (single track) into woodlands to rejoin B862. This road was also originally by Wade (1726) but proved too exposed in winter on the stretches nearer Inverness. Evidence of this flurry of military activity seems everywhere in the landscape. At **WHITE-BRIDGE** a handsome Wade bridge—on your left—has been restored, close by the Whitebridge Hotel which is itself a 'Kingshouse'—one of a chain of formerly 'official' inns, perhaps the 18C equivalent of motorway service areas.

South of Whitebridge, the road runs with military precision and gains height for an outstanding viewpoint, at over 1,200ft (372m), of the Monadhliath. Great waves of moorland rise to the east, while more distant hills on the spine of Scotland beckon to the north-west. Then the route drops past attractive Loch Tarff and descends further through scattered woods and rough grazing. By now you should be adept at spotting signs of the old road, occasionally to be noted as an overgrown track in the adjacent heathery pasture. There are glimpses of the spires and rooftops of **FORT AUGUSTUS** through the plantations as the road continues to lose height, though if you park and climb on the heathery slopes on your left, you can take your photograph clear of conifer-tops. Minutes later, down in the glen, there is a fine low-level end-on view of Loch Ness looking north.

Together with Fort William to the south and a garrison at Inverness (in an earlier Fort George), Fort Augustus was part of a chain of military settlements intended to keep the Highlands in check. The Jacobite clans captured it during the 1745 rebellion. Later, the fort was rebuilt as a Benedictine Abbey and boys' school. The Caledonian Canal also runs through this lochside community, by way of an entertaining series of locks, always a pleasure to idle beside.

In Fort Augustus, at the junction of B862 with the main A82, go right if you want to see the locks, otherwise your route is to the left and south-wards, sharing the glen, quite wide at this point, with the canal on your right. On your way down to the turning at Spean Bridge you can contemplate the great fault line along which you travel. Granites at Foyers match those at Strontian in Ardgour, 65 miles (104km) down the glen on the opposite side, indicating the scale of the ancient earth movements which wrenched and slid sideways the top part of Scotland.

Several million years later, the fault-line lochs were linked by Thomas Telford's major work, the Caledonian Canal, first opened throughout in 1822. It was built partly as an early 'job creation' scheme when a London government realised that, unless there was work for Highlanders, the manpower losses through emigration would dry up the flow of recruits for the British army and navy.

Shortly after you pass the Well of the Seven Heads—a roadside monument and complicated grisly tale—by Loch Oich, the main road crosses the canal on a swing bridge and soon reaches Loch Lochy, on a pleasant stretch among tall trees. (Try to ignore the bald swathes and patches after timber operations on the far bank hill-slopes—a necessary but not altogether scenic note.)

At Spean Bridge, many travellers pay their respects at the dignified and poignant **Commando Memorial** whose figures gaze out over the high hills on which the Commandoes trained during the Second World War. [Enthusiasts of earlier military history can take B8004, immediately after the memorial, for two minutes' drive to look for the Wade's road emerging from a plantation and descending as a rough track across an open field to the River Spean, southwards. There, it crossed on the now-ruined **'High Bridge'** where the first skirmish of the '45 took place.] Staying on the main road, before you drop to the junction with A86, note, southwards, Ben Nevis giving a hint of the great rocky faces it keeps mostly hidden from road travellers.

Go left at the A86. Shortly afterwards, a sign for Glen Roy indicates another excursion, this time up a cul-de-sac road to see the famous **Parallel Roads**. These curious hillside terraces are the shorelines of former lochs dammed by glaciers during the last Ice Age. Continuing east on A86, there are outstanding views on the right of the 'Grey Corries', the silvery, soaring hills east of Ben Nevis, including Aonach Mor, under development for skiing.

Soon the high slopes also rearing to your left become Creag Meagaidh ('Meggie'), its awesome mural cliffs out of sight from the road and popular with climbers. It is now a National Nature Reserve and fends off various bids to blanket parts of its slopes with alien forestry. Most of A86 is a good road, though there are intermittent narrow sections further east— take care. It can make a good 'escape' road to drier Speyside, should the far west be under the clouds.

You meet the young Spey at Laggan and A86 continues to **NEWTONMORE**, one of Strathspey's many small resorts. In modern tourism terms you are now in Spey Valley, the tourism authorities having decided that the common and useful Scots word 'strath' (a broad river valley) should be translated for the benefit of visitors. Perhaps Mount Nevis will be next! Newtonmore claims to be the place where the pastime of pony-trekking was first pursued. It also has the **Clan MacPherson Museum**.

Continue on A86 towards Kingussie. The fast A9 is across the river, on your right, while the Cairngorms rise behind, their bulk increasing as you travel north-eastwards. At **KINGUSSIE**, (say Kin-*yoosee*) the

**Highland Folk Museum**, has an extensive collection of artefacts indoors, such as furniture, costume, weapons, tools, and also has an outdoor display of great interest including a reconstructed 'black house' from Lewis, a turf-walled Highland house, and a clack mill plus larger-scale farming equipment.

Although A86 joins A9 just north-east of Kingussie, to avoid main road travel retrace your route briefly from the museum to take the pleasant B970 out of the village, passing below the A9 road bridge and close to **Ruthven Barracks**, the gaunt shell of a building on a green knowe (knoll). This also belongs to the Jacobite episodes, a Hanoverian garrison building blown up by the clansmen in 1746 immediately after the Culloden defeat.

B970 heads in a relaxed way north-east up Strathspey, with plenty of scenic woodlands and views of the rolling Monadhliath on your left. The River Spey, held in by raised banks, flows sluggishly in a marshy foreground. The river-flats of reeds and marshes are all that remains of a loch dammed by glacial material after the last Ice Age, but now silted up. The RSPB has an important wetland reserve here, Inch Marshes. Ospreys are quite often seen in the vicinity in summer. 'Inch' in this context does not mean island (Gaelic innis) but has its other Scots meaning of flat riverside ground.

The Spey finally breaks out to form Loch Insh. A minor road, left and close to the loch, goes back to Kincraig passing **Invereshie House** (05404 332) on the way. This hotel is a good example of a professionally run business, where the Scots owners have turned a former shooting lodge into a highly individual concern, welcoming and informal, with thoughtfully prepared food. If you are making this trip last more than one day, then Invereshie House is a good base for exploring Speyside.

Beyond Loch Insh, you cross the River Feshie by a picturesque bridge and continue to Inshriach. Here, alpine plant enthusiasts will linger over the hardy varieties at the **Inshriach Nursery** (Jack Drake), in the sheltering woodlands. A few minutes later, a signpost directs you right to Loch an Eilean. This has one of the finest loch settings on Speyside and is well worth the short walk from the car park to its shores—or, if you are energetic and reasonably well shod, the walk round its banks. Call at the converted cottage (mind the low door), now a visitor centre run by the Nature Conservancy Council, for information on the local wildlife specialities, including crested tits and crossbills. On your stroll, look for the ruined castle on a wooded islet, once a 15C Mackintosh stronghold. With tall Scots pines—note the red limbs

*Osprey*

high up—juniper and blaeberry in shaggy carpets and a rising hill-mass hinting of Arctic heights beyond, this is Speyside at its uncluttered best.

Back on B970, by way of contrast, you soon reach the junction with the broad road linking **AVIEMORE** with the ski developments which have made so much impact upon the fragile high plateau to the east. From a quiet junction on the Highland Railway, Aviemore became, from the 1960s onwards, a kind of well-chilled Benidorm with birch trees—though it was originally intended to be a St Moritz-type of upmarket development. However, plans are currently under way to smarten up its faintly seedy image and give it even greater appeal. Concrete brutality or not, amongst the slabs and boxes of the Aviemore Centre's environment, you will certainly find a good range of hotel accommodation, places to eat, discos, as well as craft, gift, book, outdoor equipment and provisions shops. It also has good sports and leisure facilities, for example, swimming, skating, curling, cinema, and it is an important local employer, though the trades-folk here annually agonise over the arrival (or not) of snow for skiing and depend on this meteorologically marginal activity to extend the visitor season. Away from the bright lights of the Aviemore Centre, close to the ski access road and hence noted first on this route, are a number of other attractions—simply read the signs—such as the **Whisky Centre**, the **Rothiemurchus Visitor Centre** and the **Fish Farm and Fishing Centre**.

Unless you are visiting Aviemore—and you probably should—go right at the junction, then shortly left at Coylumbridge. This is still the B970. The road passes by Loch Pityoulish, a kettle-hole loch, that is, one made by the melting of a huge ice-block. There are intermittent glimpses of the broadening Spey, as well as some cultivation amongst the birch thickets all the way to the junction at **BOAT OF GARTEN**.

By taking the left turn and crossing the bridge which replaced the original boat, this peaceful settlement is only moments away. You may suddenly get a nostalgic whiff of smoky steam; this is the terminus of the **Strathspey Railway**, a volunteer-run preserved line linking the village with Aviemore. Next to it is the popular golf course, while adjacent to the atmospherically restored station is the **Boat Hotel** (047983 258), a four-square, granite and typically rural old station hotel establishment. Its comfortable lounge bar serves efficient bar meals in a pleasant environment and the accommodation is also of a high standard.

Boat of Garten village is also close to the summer residence of Scotland's most famous **ospreys**, signed right, at Loch Garten off the B970 beyond the Boat junction. If you missed the other exotica of crested tits and crossbills at Loch an Eilean, you might see them here, in the chunks of the old natural Caledonian pine forest in the care of the RSPB.

By now, you will have realised that this upper part of Speyside, away from the A9, is dawdling country. From Newtonmore to Grantown-on-Spey (and beyond) there is a great swathe of countryside of high scenic value. At Boat of Garten, you are within easy reach of the A9 and hence a

*Strathspey Railway*

speedy return to Inverness, though read your map carefully for the nearest access points to the 'new' road. However, you may care to extend this route by the B970, passing through Nethy Bridge, and enjoying peaceful river and dark pine wood views all the way to **GRANTOWN-ON-SPEY**, reaching it by going left at the B970/A95 junction.

This well-laid-out little town, sturdy and glittering in Victorian grey granite, makes an interesting contrast to Aviemore's architecture. If not exiting from upper Speyside here for the delights of whisky country and the 'Moray Riviera', then continue on A95 west, along the other bank of the Spey to Dulnain Bridge. The nearby **Heather Nursery** at Skye of Curr (up a minor road off A95) offers a bewildering choice of *Calluna* and *Erica* varieties, flowering at all seasons, and you can have a cup of tea there as well.

Your main route is on A938 to reach **CARRBRIDGE**, another of the little 'satellite' resorts dependent on the summer and winter visitor activities hereabouts. The **Landmark Visitor Centre** was a pioneering and modern approach to presenting history and entertainment for visitors. There is a permanent exhibition, plus audio/visual show, as well as the Scottish Forestry Heritage Centre. You can also expect all the paraphernalia of an operation highly geared for visitors: craft and bookshop, restaurant, nature and treetop trails and all kinds of children's delights.

A938 joins the main A9 beyond Carrbridge and you can make a fast journey back to Inverness. Note on the way, **Slochd Summit**, where road and rail builders used a glacier's meltwater channel breaching the domed hills of the Monadhliath. It still carries today's traffic to over 1,300ft (400m).

# 3 THE NORTHERN HIGHLANDS
## Above the Great Glen

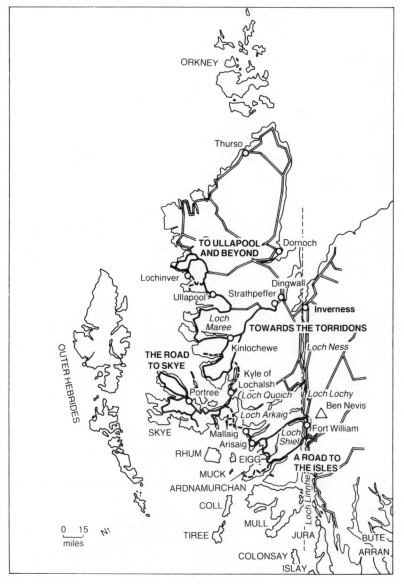

ORKNEY

Thurso

**TO ULLAPOOL AND BEYOND**

Dornoch

Lochinver

Dingwall

Ullapool

Strathpeffer

**Inverness**

*Loch Maree*

**TOWARDS THE TORRIDONS**

**THE ROAD TO SKYE**

Kinlochewe

*Loch Ness*

OUTER HEBRIDES

Kyle of Lochalsh

Portree

*Loch Quoich*

*Loch Lochy*

Ben Nevis

*Loch Arkaig*

SKYE

Mallaig

*Loch Shiel*

Arisaig

Fort William

RHUM

EIGG

**A ROAD TO THE ISLES**

MUCK

ARDNAMURCHAN

*Loch Linnhe*

COLL

MULL

0  15  N↑

miles

TIREE

JURA

BUTE

ARRAN

COLONSAY

ISLAY

With a chain of lochs in a deep glacial trench all but splitting Scotland from east coast to west, the Great Glen makes a convenient southern boundary for the mainly Highland territory described in this section. Beyond is essential Scotland—the open, empty lands fought and lamented over, the austere mountains stirring the hearts of exiles, as well as bus-trippers and well-heeled southerners getting out of the rat-race. Here are the wildest landscapes in Britain, with hills named by the Norsemen. The grandeur of the Torridon Hills, the weird peaks of the Inverpolly Forest or the shattered pinnacles of the Cuillins of Skye are just a few aspects of the landscape which certainly inspire.

## A Road to the Isles

*1 day/110 miles (176km)/from Fort William*

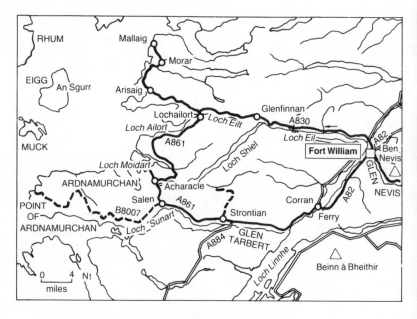

A wee bird cam tae oor haa door
He warbled sweet and early,
But aye the outcam o his sang
Was wae's me for Prince Chairlie.

William Glen (1789–1824)

There is no point in trying to hide the fact that this part of the West Highlands is one of the wettest areas in Scotland. Fortunately, the rain can be very localised—try another place 3 miles (5km) along the glen, or head for the seacoast for improvement. May, June and, perhaps, September are recommended. While copious rainfall might not suit the visitor, the loch-glitter and the washed and polished colours of the West Highland landscapes under sun depend on mild rain for their brightness. Choose your day well for this route into the hills of the far west, once trodden by that luckless figure of Scottish romance, Prince Charles Edward Stuart.

**FORT WILLIAM**, taking its name from the most southerly of the former Great Glen garrisons, is not a pretty place. However, what it lacks in grace it makes up for in sheer practicality—from fast film to fast food, supermarkets to superglue, this is the West Highland commercial centre. Its tourist information centre in Cameron Square is particularly well stocked and there is a good range of bookshops and outdoor equipment stores. The **West Highland Museum** has interesting background information on the Jacobite prince and among other diversions, the **Scottish Crafts and Ben Nevis Exhibition** is popular and will help fill a wet day. The very best aspect of the town is its nearness to **Glen Nevis**, signed left, from the roundabout at the north end of the town. This cul-de-sac route is unfair to drivers who will find their eyes stray from the bending road to ogle the soaring slopes and high grey screes of the alpine landscape. An excursion up the glen to view the flanks of the Mamores can take an hour or so—or all day if you want to walk—and thus could be separated from the whole-day trip westwards outlined below.

Take A82 north out of Fort William, then go left on A830, signed Mallaig. The first part of the drive is through surprisingly industrial and workaday environs (including the Corpach Pulp Mill) but soon the housing drops behind, leaving only the road and railway running level

*The Glenfinnan Monument*

along the banks of Loch Eil. There are fine views of **Ben Nevis** behind, with hints of the rugged profile it entirely hides from Fort William and Glen Nevis.

The main road climbs gently into the hills and away from the herons on the seaweedy flats at the end of Loch Eil. The **Glenfinnan Monument** a few minutes further on is a popular stopping-off point. The monument is actually best seen from the train, where it stands pencil-thin before a series of great hill triangles tipping into the receding loch. This is the country associated with Prince Charles Edward Stuart, the Young Pretender, the Young Chevalier or, familiarly, Bonnie Prince Charlie. On the fields at the north end of Loch Shiel, he came ashore in 1745 to raise his standard and rally the clans. Controversy sometimes breaks out as to the exact spot, but the monument itself, a curious stone lighthouse with a kilted figure on top, is a popular stroll. The NTS's Visitor Centre above the road tells the story of his rash adventure.

If all this 'Wae's me for Chairlie-ism' leaves you uncomfortable, then you can always admire the nearby West Highland Line's Glenfinnan viaduct, its graceful 21-span 1,248ft (390m) sweep dwarfed by the slopes above. The line's contractor Robert MacAlpine ('Concrete Bob') pioneered the use of mass concrete for the viaducts and bridges of the 'Mallaig extension' opened in 1901. For several years ScotRail have operated wildly popular steam-hauled regular services over this route, using steam locomotives hired, ironically, from a variety of preservation bodies.

The road continues through birchwoods and bog myrtle—the wiry shrub growing in wet places. (It has a fragrant scent when crushed—try it with pork chops.) Continue past Loch Eilt, noting Lochailort, with the road junction you will take on your return from Mallaig, and tidal Loch Ailort with its unexpected orange seaweed fringe. The road here was formerly single track, but each succeeding season brings a rash of further cutting and blasting to make a new improved highway. The Prince's Cairn by the shores of Loch nan Uamh (Gaelic: cave, pronounced 'oo-am') marks the spot where he left Scotland, broken and defeated in 1746, never to return. Between April, and the defeat at the Battle of Culloden, and September, when he was finally taken off, he had wandered the Highlands with a price of £30,000 on his head—but no Highlander betrayed him.

The road heads into the woods to reach **ARISAIG**. This little settlement is the departure point for Murdo Grant's **MV** *Shearwater* which operates a regular summer service to the Small Isles. Depending on the day you choose, you can visit a permutation of these islands: the tiny emerald chip of Muck, Eigg with its distinctive high rocky tooth of the 'Sgurr', or Rhum, island of red deer and strange Norse-named peaks.

For its size, Arisaig is also well-endowed with quality accommodation and places to eat, including the widely praised **Arisaig House** (06875 822), country-style with terraced gardens; the **Arisaig Hotel** (06875 210), a former 18C coaching inn with a 'Taste of Scotland' restaurant; also the **Old Library Lodge & Restaurant** (06875 651).

Beyond Arisaig the road goes over the headland and eventually to the coast by the far-famed white sands of **Morar**. These are better appreciated in the quiet season, their dazzling popularity tending to clutter them in high season—though in the West Highlands 'cluttered' is a relative term. Their whiteness comes from the high mica content in the local rock.

At Morar, you may wish to divert a few minutes east to view Loch Morar. Having started the day at Scotland's highest mountain, you are now at Scotland's deepest loch, at more than 1,000ft (304m). Morar was a focus of interest during the monster-hunting mania of the 1960s and 1970s, as a similar phenomenon to the one at Loch Ness was reported here. Like all good Scottish monsters, however, Morar's frequency of performance was in inverse proportion to the numbers of cameras around at the time.

**MALLAIG**, the end of the road and railway, does not itself specialise in the picturesque—even if this expectation may have been set up by the high-grade scenery of the route. However, it makes an excellent gateway for round trips to Skye (i.e. Mallaig–Armadale then Kyleakin–Kyle of Lochalsh) and other sea excursions are available from its active fishing harbour, particularly northwards to the sealochs Hourn and Nevis in all but roadless Knoydart.

Retrace your route past the glittering sands, through the birch and oaks of Arisaig and return to Lochailort to take A861 (right) by Loch Ailort, noting the fish farming cages which have taken to the water throughout the Highland lochs, both fresh and salt. Though a question-mark hangs over their environmental effects and some of the methods used by some operators to keep off predators such as herons, seals and otters, the industry brings much-needed local employment—even if it now features in the foreground of many a picture-postcard lochscape! In any case, the next looping section still offers some of the very finest of West Highland scenery.

On the approaches to the mouth of Loch Ailort, there are plenty of parking places amongst the boulders and bracken with outstanding seaward views of the Small Isles, where **Eigg** is a low island with the prominent bump of An Sgurr and **Rhum** glowers cloud-capped behind it. Then the road climbs south, across a heathery headland and drops to the sandy tidal reaches of Loch Moidart. Shortly after there is a single-track section with the road climbing another 'bealach' (Gaelic: pass) giving views over the Ardnamurchan peninsula before dropping again to the mossy wetlands of the idling Loch Shiel, slowly narrowing into a river reluctant to reach the sea. In fact, the loch only missed being a fjord by about 20ft (6m) in height and a dump of glacial material.

Before crossing the River Shiel and reaching the ribbon settlement of **ACHARACLE**, take a right turn down a narrow road overhung by lichened trees to reach **Castle Tioram** at the road end. Formerly the home of the chief of the MacDonalds of Clan Ranald, the last chief burned the castle to prevent its falling into the hands of his enemies the Campbells during the 1715 Jacobite rebellion. The square keep stands eyeless on a brackeny green islet, anchored to the mainland by a sand-spit, a shell-strewn back-to-back beach in the quiet waters of Loch Moidart's south channel.

Having returned to the main road, through the dark woodlands beyond Acharacle, you reach Salen on the well-clothed shores of Loch Sunart, another long sealoch. The single-track B8007, with blind bends in places amongst the rhododendron thickets, leads on to the most westerly headland in the British mainland, **Ardnamurchan Point**, with its lighthouse and cliffs. Out beyond the coastal woodlands, the Ardnamurchan peninsula is an area of complex crags and ridges formed by ancient volcanic activity. There are hidden beaches of white sands in the far west, worth exploring if time permits.

If you go east, remaining on A861, a slow road through the soft green woodlands, with loch views glittering on your right, eventually leads to **STRONTIAN**. This settlement gave its name to the element strontium and was a formerly important lead-mining area. If you take the time to drive up the cul-de-sac road going north from the village, there are all kinds of (to the amateur) mysterious-looking rocks to pick over! For once in the Highlands, the glen behind that part of Strontian on the main road is well settled and cultivated. There are craft workers (including a guitar maker) to detain you here.

At the very end of Loch Sunart, where A884 leads off, right, across Morvern to give a worthwhile back-door route to Mull, A861 improves to double-track again and it is a fast run through Glen Tarbert for a sight of the ridgeback of Beinn a' Bheithir (pronounced roughly Ben a Veer) near Ballachulish across Loch Linnhe.

From Inversanda up to Corran, the little bays and islets of the great seaway of Loch Linnhe often shelter rafts of sea-duck (mergansers and their kin) to interest birdwaters. At **Corran**, take the short ferry crossing, a frequent service, as a quick way back via A82 to Fort William.

# The Road to Skye

*3 days (on the island)/at least 170miles (272km)/from Kyleakin*

> *For all is rocks at random thrown,*
> *Black waves, bare crags, and banks of stone.*
>
> from *The Lord of the Isles*
> Sir Walter Scott after visiting Coruisk, Skye

For sheer drama in the landscape, Skye is matched by few other places. Under cloudless skies it is as magical as every postcard and tourism brochure have led you to expect. The notched teeth and ridges of the Cuillin Hills are tantalising from every angle. Driving on the island is straightforward, with the Kyle of Lochalsh–Kyleakin ferry frequent and non-bookable. There is also a longer crossing—Mallaig to Armadale, which links up with the 'Road to the Isles' route on p. 80.

From the **Kyleakin** terminal, A850 towards Portree starts gently enough. It runs along raised beaches with fine sea views northwards towards Applecross on the mainland and the islands of Scalpay and Raasay in the Inner Sound. At Broadford, make a mental note of the A881, for a later excursion to the Cuillins. Meanwhile it is the eastern Red Hills which catch the eye, particularly the looming scree-streaked hump of Beinn na Caillich, built in red granite, beyond Broadford.

These granitic bouldery hills continue by the road all the way to **SLIGACHAN**. Note on the way, at Luib on the shores of Loch Ainort, the **Old Skye Crofter's House**, a traditional thatched dwelling furnished in 19C style. To reach Sligachan the main road beyond the head of the

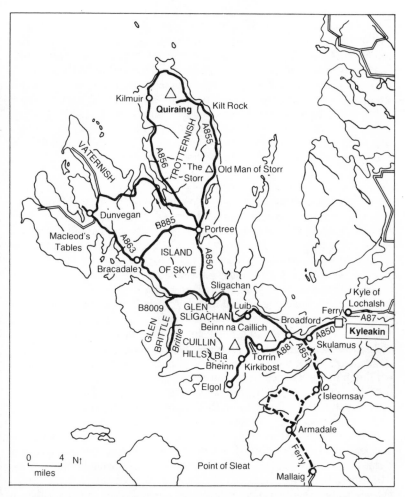

loch climbs the moors below the reddish runnelled hill mass of Glamaig, past the Raasay ferry terminal to reach the next sea inlet, Loch Sligachan. The Cuillins proper come into view. Below the buttressed spire of Sgurr nan Gillean which draws the eye, at the head of this loch, is a road junction, the Sligachan Hotel and little else except a beckoning view south down Glen Sligachan with the stark and rounded Red Hills facing the ridgy Cuillins, each made silvery against the light. Stay on A850. You now turn away from the Cuillins and the easy road runs on to Portree.

Busy with shoppers both visitor and resident, **PORTREE** is the largest settlement in Skye, yet with a population of only about 1,500. It sits around a small and sheltered bay with its own pier. There is a wide choice of accommodation. The **Coolin Hills Hotel** (0478 2003) at the far end of the little town offers superb views across the bay all the way to the distant grey notches of the Cuillins. The hotel has comfortable accommodation, pleasant food and a friendly lounge bar where pub meals are served.

Portree is a good base from which to explore the northern peninsulas of Skye of which Trotternish is the most spectacular. Take A855 northwards out of the town. Having glimpsed the granite of the Red Hills and the gabbro of the Cuillins, this route holds much scenic interest because of more volcanic rocks. Great lava flows stop short on an almost continuous cliff west of the road. In a number of places, ancient landslips along these cliffs have created spectacular shearings and pinnacles where the softer sedimentary rocks below have failed to take the weight. The first of these is seen against the skyline within a few minutes of leaving Portree.

The **Old Man of Storr**, standing below the shattered face of The Storr, can be approached via a path up and through a forestry plantation, but if time is pressing, continue northwards, past neat and careful crofts in a moorland landscape to **Kilt Rock** at Elishader. (Look for a loch on your left.) There is no escaping the geology of Skye. Hereabouts it is an attraction in itself. The size of the car park here indicates that both bus tours and free-range visitors take in this curious rock formation. On the cliff face alternate bandings of sedimentary rock with intrusive leaves of dolerite make a curious vertical pleated effect, much like a kilt. (Climbing the safety fence and walking north for a closer look is not advised. The cliff face is dangerous and you are probably trespassing. However, if you do, students of the automobile industry will be rewarded by a magnificent car dump in a hollow close by, but out of sight. The numbers of interesting derelicts scattered in the landscape make excellent subjects for photography. For some reason this endearing characteristic of Skye is never mentioned in guidebooks.

A few minutes further brings you in sight of the most spectacular of the lava landslips: the **Quiraing**. The closest point to these extraordinary rock forms is reached by going left on a minor road at Brogaig by Staffin Bay. This impressive road lifts on to the moor. The rockscape, with its intriguingly named features such as the Needle, the Prison and the Table, is high on your right. The road then tackles the line of cliffs west of the Quiraing by a series of hairpins. There is a car park on top—and, of course, magnificent views east to the mainland. The fit, well-shod and sure-footed can tackle the Quiraing itself either by walking along the clifftop (relatively easy) or, more interestingly, starting from lower down on paths north-east along the base of the cliff. This lower route takes you into the heart of the weird pinnacles, cliffs and rock sculpture.

Return to the main road at Brogaig after your car excursion to the Quiraing to go north and west for the loop along the top of Trotternish. There are many interesting coastal stretches to discover: take in the **Kilmuir Croft Museum**, a friendly place (if you fall into conversation) and a pleasing evocation of the life of a crofting township set out in a cluster of thatched buildings containing farm implements, reconstructed interiors, plus documents and photographs. Just up the road you will find the grave and monument to Flora Macdonald, romantic help-mate of

*Kilmuir Croft Museum*

Prince Charles Edward Stuart. From this breezy top end of Skye, you may wish to return on A856/A850 directly to Portree.

Another popular excursion is to Dunvegan Castle via the A850, by way of the white clustered settlements beside Loch Snizort Beag and the empty plateau-moors of Vaternish. Looking across to the most westerly part of the island, the eroded lava plateau landforms reach their greatest heights on the curious flat topped hills known as MacLeod's Tables. Set above the sea, **Dunvegan Castle** has been the seat of the chiefs of the Clan MacLeod for 700 years. As a lived-in rambling castle, it has changed greatly over the centuries. Some may even find the crenellated battlement a little comical and the general ambience inside and out rather dingy—the Scottish food and travel writer Derek Cooper refers to 'porridge-coloured stucco'—but there are some fascinating family treasures on view including the ancient 'Fairy Flag'. This banner is said to have miraculous powers of bringing victory to the clan and to be potent enough still to be used once more in time of need.

*Dunvegan*

Continue down the A863. On the way, **Dun Beag** near Bracadale is one of the best-preserved brochs on Skye. There is a signposted car park and only a short walk (uphill!) to this curious dry-walled circular structure. Scotland's unique brochs were sophisticated circular defensive towers up to 40ft (12m) high (Mousa Broch, Shetland—see p. 132), built without mortar.

Note, shortly afterwards, the B885, swinging left across country as a short-cut back to Portree. Continue south to the head of Loch Harport, then go right on B8009, soon cutting back left at a sign for **Glen Brittle**. This little road drops from the moorlands with the ramparts of the Cuillins filling the windscreen straight ahead. Down in the glen the road swings right with the great ridges rearing immediately to the east. You meet the sea by the tents and caravans at Loch Brittle. A path, which gives serious climbers access to some of the toughest peaks, runs up from the grassy campsite and provides even the ordinary pedestrian, with a little effort, some fine rocky views of the soaring ridges. (Do not attempt the peaks themselves unless experienced and properly equipped.)

Though the Glen Brittle landscapes are outstanding—and a visit to Dunvegan and Glen Brittle are probably a good day's worth—they are matched by an equally spectacular approach to the Cuillins by way of the A881 at Broadford, signed for Elgol. Glen Brittle and Elgol could also be taken as a day-long excursion, assuming you did not intend to walk far.

Thus either from Portree, or from Glen Brittle (via A863), retrace your way along A850 round the Red Hills to Broadford, going right, signed A881 for Elgol. The road leads into **Strath Suardal**, and soon goes past the ivy-clad ruins of the Kilchrist pre-Reformation kirk with its clan graves. Shortly afterwards, the purple moors, back-lit western hills, reedy loch and wading cattle may give you the strange sensation that you are travelling through a romantic Victorian oil painting suddenly come alive. If you stop for photographs in a layby by Loch Cill Chriosd, look around on the grassy banks for the uncommon flower *Dryas octopetala*, mountain avens, white-petalled with its leaves like a miniature oak. It thrives here on a limestone exposure. Probably nowhere else in Scotland can you see it from the car. You may meet it again at low level at Inchnadamph (p. 97) and near Durness in the far north—because a thin band of this limestone runs all the way up north-west Scotland, outcropping intermittently and flagged by this special plant. (Please do not pick it or, worse, dig bits up—it will not thrive for you.)

This band of limestone was converted by heat into local marble, quarried further along the road at Torrin—not just to supply the local souvenir shops with lampshade bases, but also crushed for agricultural purposes and building. Limestone means a more fertile soil, hence the woodlands along this stretch of the road. However, by this stage on your approach to Loch Slapin your eye will be drawn by the jagged bulk of Blaven (Bla Bheinn, 3,043ft/943m) on the far shore of Loch Slapin. This wild section goes by gaunt hills, round the head of the sealoch, and then by rough woods below Blaven you climb away from the lochside to Kirkibost. Beyond, on your right, you'll see the track cut by the army in 1968, amid much protest; it runs in to the Cuillin fastness at Camasunary.

**ELGOL** is the end of the road. Some claim it offers the finest view anywhere in the UK. To make the most of it you may wish to make your way—on foot—north of the road that goes down steeply to a car park. There is a track which starts on the right, partway down the final descent. It goes between the scattered houses and looks as if it stops at a croft. Instead, if you persevere for a few minutes, the route takes you on to the rough grassland. This footpath eventually runs all the way to Camasunary and Loch Coruisk (but only if you are experienced and well-shod.) Content yourself with the heart-stopping view of the back-lit, black-toothed hills with the afternoon sun glittering on the great inlet of Loch Scavaig. There is a competent 'tea-shoppie' in Elgol, where you can top up with a sticky cake before your return to Portree or Kyleakin.

[Note: You may wish to leave Skye by Armadale for Mallaig on the mainland—a summer-only service. Take A851 at Skulamus east of Broadford to traverse the peninsula of Sleat. In contrast to the acid moorlands of the first part of this road, the western side of Sleat, reached via an unclassified loop road starting beyond Isleornsay, is sometimes known as the Garden of Skye—thanks to the same rich limestones already encountered in Strath Suardal. Otherwise the main attraction is the **Clan Donald Centre and Armadale Gardens** which you will find shortly after your return to the main road. The museum is housed in a restored section of the castle and the complex also includes beautiful woodland walks, restaurant and gift shop.]

## Towards the Torridons

*1 day/(up to) 150 miles (240km)/from Strathpeffer*

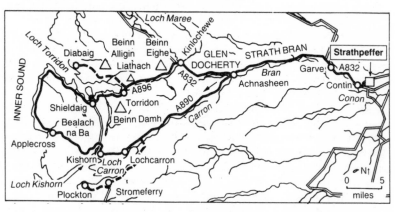

> *Loch Torridon, though very little visited, is better worth seeing than most of the Scottish sea-lochs, and it is to be regretted that the country is so wild, and the accommodation so scanty, as to preclude many tourists from approaching it.*
> Murray's Handbook for Travellers in Scotland (1894)

The Torridons are the red sandstone and pale quartz mountains in Glen Torridon—yet another glen claiming the title of the most spectacular on the mainland. Wester Ross and its austere and brooding landscapes make an adventurous excursion from Easter Ross, an area of contrast with its woods and rolling farmlands. In essence, the far west is a land of empty spaces, slightly intimidating in consequence. Perhaps part of the area's emotional appeal is the challenge of its emptiness. As a practical result, this route is far from littered with 'tea shoppies' and even your bar lunch choice is limited.

**STRATHPEFFER** takes its name from the River Peffery (Gaelic: bright or sparkling). This substantial village of solid guest houses and hotels was once styled the Harrogate of Scotland because of the efficacy of its medicinal waters, both sulphurous and chalybeate (iron-bearing). Its heyday as a spa centre came before the First World War. The old **Pump Room** survives, a photographic exhibition relates the spa story and you can still take the waters here. Vanished glories are also recalled in the renovated railway station (1885) of its long-closed branch line, now the **Strathpeffer Visitor Centre** with craft workers 'in residence'. It also offers an audio/visual programme. There is a wide choice of hotel and guest house accommodation here—the **Holly Lodge Hotel** (0997 21254) has a good local reputation for innovative cuisine.

Go west to join the A832 at Contin. Only a mile or two beyond, the **Falls of Rogie** are signed—worth a stroll, as the sylvan falls are very photogenic, though you may find the suspension footbridge disconcertingly elastic. Continuing west, just by the falls signpost you leave the last of the eastern fields behind. The rising road envelopes you, very suddenly, in a Highland landscape.

Go left beyond Garve, still on A832 and over the watershed, through woodlands into Strath Bran. This is the bare backbone of Scotland, a mainly open section of hills viewed at 'arm's-length' across winding river flats southwards, while the rising ground to the right hides the remote range of the Fannichs, haunt of few but the hardiest of hillwalkers.

At Achnasheen head left and down Glen Carron. If time permits, at the junction with the A896, you can take the main A890 down the south side of Loch Carron, following the railway all the way. In 1870, the line first opened a route through this austere and unforgiving landscape as far as Stromeferry. Travelling through such a sparsely populated area it brought the new-fangled idea of uniform time with it—not a notion of concern to the locals, nor to the local stationmasters. The railway owners had to despatch from Dingwall, on the first train daily, a guard with a watch, who gave the correct time to each station as the train passed through!

The Dingwall and Skye Railway Company's real intention had been to capture the lucrative west coast fish trade. The pierhead at Strome, which you reach if you follow the south shore road, was the scene of an extraordinary incident, known half-seriously as the Battle of Strome Pier. In May 1883, with the herring season attracting east coast boats with better catching techniques than the west coast fishers, matters came to a head on the question of Sunday landings at Strome. The east coasters had no scruples about the Sabbath.

*Plockton*

Steamers from Stornoway brought the fresh fish to Strome but the locals seized the pier and prevented unloading, easily repulsing six constables and the steamer crew! Soon the matter was in the hands of the War Office in far-off London. Massive police presence and a standby troop train were needed for the protection of the Sabbath-breakers the following weekend. But the fish train was duly despatched to the London market for Monday morning. All this drama amongst the sleepy, empty hills!

The point of continuing down Loch Carron is to make your way via a minor road, right, over to **PLOCKTON** in its superb setting—unusually for the west coast—looking east up Loch Carron. Once it was a fishing settlement, now, in the style of a number of far west communities, it is a slightly antiseptic, summer cottagey kind of place, but certainly attractively clustered round the shore, with its designer roses and even palm trees enjoying the frost-free airs.

Retrace your route to the road junction at the head of Loch Carron, going left on A896 to reach the stretched-out village of **LOCH-CARRON** which has a good choice of accommodation and provision stores. A896 continues to **KISHORN**. The upper part of Loch Kishorn has a large hole in the ground, or more accurately a (former) oil platform construction yard. In the 1970s it was proposed to build this further south at Drumbuie near the railhead at Kyle. However, the NTS owned land nearby and, demonstrating an institutionalised form of the 'not in my back yard' syndrome, spent much money in resolutely opposing the development which was consequently allowed at Kishorn, a much more attractive site. At the head of the loch, below the rock buttresses of the Applecross hills, take a left for **APPLECROSS**.

This road is the variously spelled 'Bealach na Ba', the Pass of the Cattle, probably the highest public road in the UK and perhaps the only one crossing ptarmigan nesting territory. (Ptarmigan are white-winged high-altitude grouse.) You reach the high eroded plateau by a series of hairpins up the valley headwall. There are magnificent views of Skye on the descent from the stony sandstone uplands to the coastal woods of Applecross. Then make your way north and east along the coast, then the Loch Torridon shore, by a road built as recently as 1976, to join A896 (left) for **SHIELDAIG**.

Shieldaig (Norse: sild-vik—herring bay) curves neatly round a crescent bay with the tall trees of Shieldaig Island just offshore. It also has the artificially tidy air of a 'second-home' settlement. The headland due north

91

of the village makes an interesting stroll. There is a path, at first hard to find, which brings rewarding sealoch and mountain views.

The next section of A896, along Upper Loch Torridon, reveals some of Scotland's most impressive mainland mountains. **Beinn Alligin** hunches away from the prevailing westerlies, the diagonal gash on its main peak a black scar by afternoon light and the hill-scrambler's delight of the Horns of Alligin a battlemented endpiece to the main ridge. Next to it the long upturned boat-keel ridge of **Liathach** starts. By the time the head of the loch is reached—noting on the way the bar lunch possibility of the **Torridon Hotel** (044587 242)—the endless stony slopes rear up to fill the windscreen. The tiny village of **TORRIDON** (and Fasag), a typical post-Highland-Clearance coastal settlement founded after the original population was cleared from the upper glens, is squeezed between hillslope and sealoch. Here you will find the NTS **Torridon Visitor Centre**, which explains the geology and wildlife of the area.

If time permits, before seeing Glen Torridon immediately east, you may first want to follow the minor road which leads west from the visitor centre all the way to **DIABAIG**. This gives outstanding views south of the pared-down, bare-rock hills around Beinn Damh. Diabaig itself is a little settlement scattered down a steep hill which ends suddenly in a little pier. Return to the NTS Visitor Centre and take A896 into Glen Torridon.

Liathach continues to flank the glen on the left, its spires and pinnacles often cloud-swirled. Note the walker's path half-way along the glen, between Liathach and its neighbour **Beinn Eighe** (usually pronounced to rhyme with 'say'). This long complex of ridges shows great drifts and runnels of grey quartzite which at this point in the glen caps the red sandstone. The best view of all in the glen is probably in the vicinity of Loch Clair, far enough away from Liathach to appreciate its extraordinary shape.

Glen Torridon leads down to Kinlochewe and on the way you may note the sign that indicates where the NTS territory meets the Nature Conservancy Council's Beinn Eighe National Nature Reserve. **KINLOCHEWE** is a little village at the junction. The **Kinlochewe Hotel** (044854 253) has been recently modernised. The community below the grey stony slopes of Beinn Eighe is the gateway to Loch Maree (see p. 94).

The homeward route is east (right at the junction) on A832 up Glen Docherty, with its outstanding Loch Maree views from a prominent car park just below the summit of the pass. A832 leads on to Achnasheen and the return eastwards to Strathpeffer.

# To Ullapool and Beyond

*1–2 days/120 miles (192km)/from Kinlochewe to the Kylesku bridge*

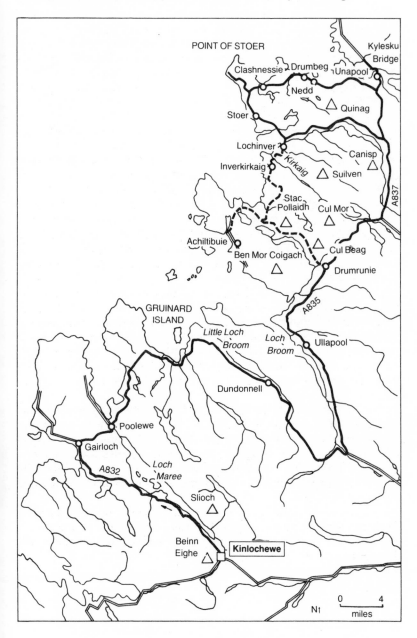

*If I could build a hundred homes and live in each a while*
*I'd build them all along the coast from Sandwood down to Kyle.*

'Sandwood down to Kyle'
song by Dave Goulder

The west and north coasts of Scotland have one main 'rim' road which is joined by a series of routes running like the spokes of a wheel from the Inverness area. The key to west coast touring if time is limited is to select a suitable part of the rim. The Torridon route (p. 89) gives a flavour of the wild hills of Wester Ross. This route has the substantial fishing settlement of Ullapool as its mid-point. Its locals claim that they can drive to Inverness in an hour (the road is double-track all the way). Visitors should take a little longer, but the A835 Inverness–Ullapool road is certainly the fastest way to and from the seas of the north-west. Also, above Ullapool note an unusual feature of the north-west: a choice of side roads! In the Highlands, difficult terrain often means one road only— 'rural byways' is not a phrase used by Highland tourist brochure copywriters. None the less, the little coastal loops between Ullapool and Lochinver provide some interesting excursions through the strange geology of the ancient Lewisian rocks.

From **KINLOCHEWE**, A832 goes north-west along the shores of **Loch Maree**. On the far shore, the mountain **Slioch** (Gaelic: spear) stands as a tall sandstone fort on its plinth of tougher rock. It guards the remote and roadless hills beyond—with their gritty and unfamiliar names, such as Mullach Coire Mhic Fhearchair 'the summit of the corrie of Farquar's son' (try 'vik-errachar') and the equally magnificently unpronounceable and hidden A' Mhaighdean 'the Maiden' (something like 'vyejen'). In Scotland treeless deer-runs and waste-lands are often called 'forests'. These peaks are in the barely glimpsed Fisherfield Forest.

Your eye is more likely to be caught by the pinewoods of the loch, especially on your left, where fragments of the ancient Caledonian pine forest survive on the slopes of Beinn Eighe and its outliers. There is an information centre on the work of the Nature Conservancy Council by the shores of the loch and a nature trail for the well-shod. Red deer are almost guaranteed, though the other local speciality, pine martens, are much harder to spot: they are rumoured to forage around the layby litter bins.

Red-limbed pine, blue loch and looming hill make the environs of Loch Maree harmonious. The scenic attractions have even survived the attentions of the 17/18C iron-masters who once shipped in Cumberland ores and smelted them with local oak. Some oak still grows here at the northern limits of its range.

After noting the short and easy footpath to the **Victoria Falls**, leave the shores of Loch Maree to reach salt water near **GAIRLOCH**. This little community with its fishing pier is a locally important centre with some shopping and eating choice, including the family-run and friendly

**Myrtle Bank Hotel** (0445 2004)—which offers cream scone teas as well as bar meals. The **Gairloch Heritage Museum** portrays the area from prehistoric times to the present day.

You may also note the localised weather patterns due to the nearness of the sea to the high hills: Gairloch golfers can enjoy a dry and breezy day on the local course as families frolic on the nearby sands. At the same time Torridon hillwalkers get drookit (Scots: soaked).

A832 crosses the headland to drop down to the next bay, the former war-time convoy assembly-point of Loch Ewe, and soon reaches the famous **Inverewe Gardens**, in the care of the NTS. These are often described as sub-tropical because of the warming effect of the Gulf Stream. The head gardener disagrees with that description, preferring the more accurate label of 'cool temperate'. Either way, the plant colonies and groupings from South America, New Zealand and other far-flung places make a stunning display. The garden's original owner, Osgood MacKenzie, transformed this previously barren headland, more than 120 years ago, with copious amounts of soil and seaweed and by planting shelter belts. Some of the oldest trees were originally planted by excavating a hole for them in solid rock! As well as managing the garden, the NTS also manage a decent cup of tea (and more substantial fare) in their restaurant. There is a well-stocked shop which even sells exotic locally cropped seeds—not for the impatient amateur.

The road lifts away from the war-time anchorage of Loch Ewe and shortly drops to the fine coastal scenery of Gruinard Bay, with its sands, raised beaches, dark hills inland and the slightly sinister presence of Gruinard Island. Only recently declared safe, this harmless green hump in the bay was chosen by faceless scientists in far-off London as a suitable site for germ warfare experiments. For decades afterwards its surface was contaminated by deadly anthrax spores. Aside from this gloomy note, Gruinard is a cheery enough place in sunshine.

Cross the next headland and descend east alongside the crofts of Little Loch Broom. Past the fish cages, hopeful herons and orange low-tide wrack at the end of the loch you will find the old-established and welcoming **Dundonnell Hotel** (085483 204). Beyond that there is a stretch of woodland, though the road soon rises past broken rocky cliffs and on to a sombre stretch of moor. This is 'Destitution Road,' built in 1851. By that time potatoes had replaced oats as a staple in many Highland communities. Crop failure meant starvation and the road was one of a number of Highland projects initiated to give work to starving men. Some say they were paid with food only. The road gives a magnificent view, behind and to the north-west, of An Teallach, 'the forge', with its terraced sandstone humps and ridges.

Continue down to the Braemore junction with the main Ullapool road, A835. Go left and down into woodland. The site of the **Corrieshalloch Gorge** is unmistakable—a large car park and toilets are on the right. Across the road, paths lead through the trees to the spindly suspension bridge and vertigo-inducing viewpoints of the Falls of Measach which cascade about 200ft (62m) into a narrow gorge. The gorge was probably cut by meltwaters from glaciers in comparatively recent times, geologically speaking.

A835 then runs smoothly and speedily down to the shores of Loch Broom, giving glimpses of the white houses of **ULLAPOOL** ahead. The British Fisheries Society, in an attempt to exploit the local herring stocks, built a large fishing station, a planned settlement for fishermen and other workers, here in 1788. The grid street-plan survives and Ullapool is still important for its fishery. (It is also the ferry port for Stornoway in the Outer Hebrides.) Very often Eastern Bloc factory ships are in the bay, these 'Klondykers' buying direct from Scottish vessels. The foreign crews strolling around give the community a cosmopolitan air—helped, in the main season, by several late-opening shops. As the main centre in the north-west, the accommodation choice is very wide, including the well-known **Ceilidh Place** (0854 2103) with two levels of accommodation in its own inimitable and non-conforming style. This unexpected establishment also runs its own restaurant and coffee house, offering wholefoods and sensible menus long before it became fashionable. As its name suggests, it also features performing artistes of various persuasions.

Northwards, towards and into Sutherland, lie some of the most distinctive—not necessarily the same as the most picturesque—landforms in the UK. You can reach them by staying on the fast and open A835/A837 all the way to Lochinver, the next settlement of any size northwards. If time permits you may want to keep the fast road for your return and instead go north of Ullapool, past the long wall of Ben Mor Coigach across Loch Canaird, as far as a lonely junction at Drumrunie. Go left here, signed Achiltibuie. The road takes you below the crumbling pinnacles of **Stac Pollaidh**, just to the north. This impossibly shaped palisade of splintered sandstone makes an interesting scramble for the experienced. That much of its rockwork is unstable will be quite obvious on close inspection.

The less energetic will prefer to follow the road through a bare landscape to a junction where, going straight on, a cul-de-sac road leads to the strung-out settlement of **ACHILTIBUIE**, facing the bleak Summer Isles. The village has an enterprising **Smoke-house** and a **Hydroponicum** where exotic fruits grow in a space-age garden, encapsulated from the prevailing south-westerlies.

Alternatively, at this far-flung junction turn right and north for Lochinver via some outstanding coastal and hill views. Take your time here as the road is single-track with more than the occasional blind bend. The landscape over which you travel is essentially a carved and gouged out platform of ancient rock (Lewisian gneiss) on which oddly shaped hills like herded beasts are crouched, carved out of the old red sandstone. Spend any time in the area and you will come to recognise the strange far north-west litany of Ben Mor Coigach, Stac Pollaidh, Cul Beag, Cul Mor, Suilven, Canisp and Quinag—certainly not the highest hills in Scotland but of a character, changing with light and direction of view, out of all proportion to their size.

On the way north, as you descend in woodland to the River Kirkaig, look for the road going right immediately after the river bridge. There is a picnic area by the river. Just on the bend is a track leading up to what might be Scotland's most remote bookshop. **Achins Bookshop** is a well-established browser's delight. (The adjacent track by the river goes a long, long way in to the hill Suilven.) A few minutes later **LOCHINVER** is reached. This has a fishing pier and when the fleet is operating from here the village can be surprisingly busy. Here the peak of **Suilven**, from the south a steep and sinuous ridge, is suddenly revealed as a dramatic pillar, looming end-on and best seen from the cul-de-sac Baddidarach road. (Go left at the top end of the village.) Lochinver is a haven in the midst of this bare-bone, loch-linked landscape. Remember there is a good double-track road back to Inverness if you should suddenly yearn for soft fields!

For further exploration, head north on A837 from the village, taking B869, a single-track road, left, signed Stoer and Clashnessie. There are more mountainous views in the driver's mirror on this attractive little road which goes past sandy bays at Clachtoll and Stoer. Soon a minor road, left again, leads down all the way to the lighthouse at **Point of Stoer**. A clifftop walk northwards for about 2 miles (3km) from the light-house car park over moorland pasture by the cliff edge leads to the **Old Man of Stoer**, an impressive flaky red sandstone seastack near Point of Stoer. Returning to B869, continue your circuit via Clashnessie, with more white sands, then east towards **Drumbeg**.

You may wish to pause, perhaps for lunch, at the **Drumbeg Hotel** (05713 236), popular with fishermen. By this point, the views across a jumble of bays and islands, and also to the long wall of the mountain **Quinag**, are constantly improving. The next short section of the road, past Nedd, will need more than the usual concentration from the driver, not just because of distracting views, but because of a particularly interesting hairpin bend and steep hill close to Loch Nedd. This road is not difficult, just a little adventurous. The single track section joins the main A894 south of the fine bridge over Kylesku, which leads to further adventures in the far north.

There are also a number of points of interest on the A837/A835 main road back to Ullapool. These include the gaunt ruins of Ardvreck Castle, built in the late 15C by the MacLeods, on an island on Loch Assynt. A little further south at **Inchnadamph**, the Traligill Burn disappears and re-appears in a series of limestone caves and pots. Botanists will also enjoy the interesting local flora. Nature interest is also sustained at the **Knockan Cliff Nature Trail** below Ledmore junction.

# TOURING THE ISLANDS

Skye (p. 84) and Shetland (p. 131) have been treated in detail but excellent driving routes can be put together for many other islands.

## Orkney

Only 6 miles (10km) at their nearest point from the Scottish mainland, this low-lying cluster of green islands offers archaeological sites in variety, plus abundant birdlife and, in places, spectacular coastal scenery. Highlights include **St Magnus Cathedral**, **Earl Patrick's** and the **Bishop's Palace** in KIRKWALL; the **Maes Howe** burial chamber; the former naval anchorage and scuttling place of the German First World War naval fleet at **Scapa Flow**; the **Italian Chapel** (made from scrap metal and other discarded material by POWs) at Lambholm; the **Ring of Brogar** standing stones, plus a selection of museums and island trips. **Ferry**: from Scrabster, near Thurso, or (shorter, non-bookable) from John o' Groats (see p. 99).

## The Outer Hebrides

The Western Isles consist of **Lewis and Harris** (one island), then **North Uist**, **Benbecula** and **South Uist** (joined by causeways). Further south is **Barra** and a tailing-off of small islands beyond. This is the stronghold of the Gaelic language, a land of empty white beaches and white crofts, of blue lochs in brown moor and of green coastal grazings. The islands' strung-out shape means that quite long tours can be worked out. Places of interest include Historic Scotland's **Lewis Black House**, a traditional island dwelling; **Balranald and Loch Druidibeg Nature Reserves**; **Callanish Standing Stones**, plus a variety of other early religious and prehistoric sites. The Western Isles represent a 'get-away-from-it-all' and very relaxed style of touring holiday, where you will fit in with the local pace of life. **Ferry**: connections from Ullapool and Uig on Skye.

## Mull

Sometimes known, rather unkindly, as 'the Officers' Mess' because of the number of retired military men from the south who have set up home there, Mull certainly conforms to the non-Scot's idea of a romantic island. It is possible to tour there for a long weekend and not meet any inhabitant who was born north of Manchester. Wide accommodation choice and plenty of attractions to make a tour interesting including **Torosay** and **Duart Castles**, the little island of **Iona**, the **Old Byre Heritage Centre**, as well as spectacular coastal scenery in the west. **Ferries**: from Oban or, worth considering as non-bookable and cheaper, Lochaline to Fishnish.

## Islay and Jura

A most interesting contrast of islands: Islay is active with whisky distilling and farming and still has a sense of community and of ordinary folk going about their business. Main points of interest include the **Museum of Islay**

*Machrie Moore Standing Stones, Arran*

Life, the superb **Kildalton Cross** as well as fine coastal scenery, especially around Loch Gruinart (RSPB). Distillery visiting is also possible and there is a good accommodation choice. Jura by contrast has one road, one village, few people, wild scenery and lots of red deer. **Ferry**: from Kennacraig on West Loch Tarbert to Islay. Five minute crossing from Port Askaig (Islay) to Jura.

## Arran
The Clyde coast holiday and outdoor island—the ferry is full of Glasgow folk wearing walking boots! Spectacular mountain scenery, interesting coastline. **Brodick Castle and Country Park** and the **Arran Heritage Museum** are also of interest. There is a wide accommodation choice of which the **Auchranny Country House Hotel** (0770 2234/2235) in Brodick is probably the most up-market. **Ferry**: from Ardrossan.

## Scotland's Smaller Islands
There is a wide choice of smaller islands, from **Bute** to **Coll and Tiree** and beyond, the most attractive of which might be **Colonsay**, with its wide variety of habitat in a small area. You can just about justify bringing a car on the ferry from Oban (or via Islay), but bicycles ought to be sufficient. The island's only hotel, the **Isle of Colonsay Hotel** (09512 316) is an excellent base. Sunday night is always fresh oyster night. Finally, the Small Isles, **Rhum**, **Eigg**, **Muck** and **Canna**, though not car-touring territory, are an interesting diversion on the Fort William to Mallaig route described on p. 81. **Ferry**: from Mallaig or contact Murdo Grant, Arisaig, Inverness-shire (06875 219 or 224).

## Ferry Timetables
Obtainable for the above islands from Caledonian MacBrayne Ltd, The Ferry Terminal, Gourock, Renfrewshire (0475 33755).

## Orkney Ferry Services
P&O Ferries, Orkney & Shetland Services, Jamieson's Quay, Aberdeen (Scrabster/Stromness reservations 0856 85065/6). Also Orkney Ferries, Burwick Terminal, South Ronaldsay, Orkney (085683 348).

# 4 NORTH-EAST SCOTLAND
## Around the Grampians

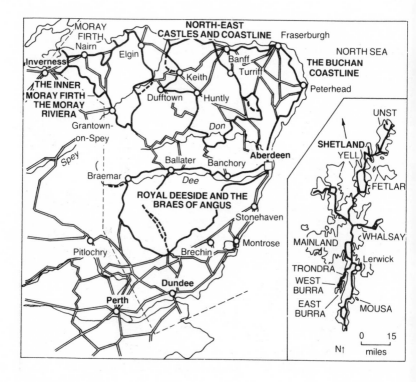

The geological barrier of the Highland Boundary Fault runs up from the Central Highlands towards the North Sea and meets the coast at Stonehaven. The north-eastern wedge of Highland hills is often called the Grampians. Yet it does not mean that everything beyond the line is 'Highland'. In the east, a comparatively low-lying coastal strip of land runs up from Angus into the old county of Aberdeenshire, then turns west along the Moray Firth coast through the former counties of Banff and Moray.

Sometimes the area north and east of the hills is known as the 'Grampian cocoon'—sheltered not just from the worst of the rain-bearing south-westerlies, but also in former times from southern influences, creating self-contained communities. Its roots are partly in the land, even before the time of the great improving landlords showed how to strip away the moor and lime it to give richer pastures, and partly by the sea, where a whole chain of tough granite settlements owe their livelihood to the local fishery. The north-east is neither Highland nor Lowland, though it contains elements of both.

Note that Shetland is included in this section. With a Scandinavian rather than a Gaelic heritage, it certainly does not belong to the Highlands. Aberdeen, its ferry-port, is its mainland Scotland gateway—and hence its inclusion here as a natural extension to touring in the north-east.

## Royal Deeside and the Braes of Angus

*1–2 days (at least) 140 miles (224km)/from Aberdeen*

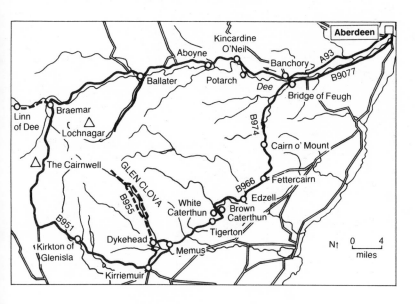

Busk, oh busk bonnie lassie,
Aye, and come awa wi me,
And I'll tak ye tae Glen Isla,
Near bonnie Glen Shee.

Traditional

Busk is Scots for 'prepare' or 'get dressed' and as you busk for this route, remember to throw in a stout pair of shoes, in case one of the glens, forest trails or riverbanks tempts you. This is hill country, great domed masses cut by long glens which offer interesting walks even at low levels. The general name for these long hills south of the Dee river valley was formerly the Mounth, from Gaelic Monadh, moorland hills. From the south—the broad vale of Strathmore in Angus—ancient routes run across this hill barrier to the north-east. These Mounth tracks were used in their day by armies, including perhaps the Roman legions, as well as by cattle-drovers, packmen and traders. These through-routes are still walked today, but only three motoring roads cross the heathery fastnesses. Your route uses two of them, out of and back to Deeside. You *can* do the route in one day, but there are a lot of points of interest.

Leave **ABERDEEN** (see p. 108) by the A93 North Deeside Road, which starts as Great Western Road (off Holburn Street) within the city boundary. This leads by way of a well-heeled commuter belt taking in Cults, Bieldside (the 'bield' part is Scots for shelter) and Milltimber into open country beyond Peterculter. Look right when crossing the bridge at the far end of Peterculter: well away from his normal Trossachs range, a technicolour Rob Rob Macgregor statue stands on the edge of the rocky river.

In this well-wooded farming country, the hills are still gentle and the River Dee runs on your left; it is more easily seen from the South Deeside Road, an alternative route to Banchory. However, by way of compensation, you will soon see a sign for **Drum Castle** (NTS), the first of many on this stretch. Drum, a venerable 13C tower house with later additions, has rounded corners to withstand battering ram attack. Note that most NTS properties have grounds open all day, all year, so you can at least always see the setting.

17C **Crathes Castle** is just a little further west, with a delightful series of small-scale yew-hedged gardens all around, in addition to its notable interior with painted ceilings. The well-scrubbed little town of **BAN-CHORY**, only minutes beyond, is popular with Sunday strollers from

*Crathes Castle*

Aberdeen. The **Brig o' Feugh** (pronounced initially like 'feud' but with Scots 'ch'), on the South Deeside Road, spans a foaming river where salmon leap—locally speaking 'loup'—in season.

The main A93 continues its course for the well-clothed hills, climbing gently with beech hedges, pale-trunked birches and posing pheasants by field-edges. At **Potarch** an attractive picture-postcard stone bridge of 1814 spans the Dee. **Kincardine o' Neil's** ruined kirk (1233) by the road was built as a hospice for travellers on the crossroads with one of the

Mounth tracks from the south. The resort community of **ABOYNE** (mostly designed by a Manchester banker in the 1890s) is laid out in grey granite around the village green, setting for its Highland Games.

It is beyond Aboyne that the Highland flavour begins to predominate. One of the most attractive stretches is near Cambus o' May, at the Muir (moor) of Dinnet, with its birch trees on a purplish tweedy cloth—you are now in shortbread-tin-illustration country, but none the less attractive for all that! You may feel that the carved legend on a roadside granite boulder here: 'You are now entering the Highlands', is not really necessary.

**BALLATER** is an integral part of the Royal Deeside business. Many of its shops bear the legend 'By Royal Appointment'. Even ordinary folk can buy the same brown bread they eat up the road at Balmoral! (Very tasty—treacle is thought to be the interesting extra ingredient!) A place of resort, because of its curative wells, even before Victoria discovered the area, Ballater was important not just as a provisioning point for the Royals' summer home, but also as the terminus of the Deeside Railway, which vanished in the 1960s. The handsome station building survives with part of it housing the tourist information centre and a small Great North of Scotland Railway display. Ballater not only has the attractions of a cosy and neat little community; it is in the centre of increasingly impressive scenery.

There is a wide choice of accommodation in Ballater. If you want to sample one of Scotland's most sophisticated leisure developments then try the **Craigendarroch Hotel and Country Club** (03397 55858). There are a few other country house hotels as comfortable and there are a very few other hotels with something like the range of leisure options—but nowhere else in Scotland has combined the two elements so successfully. By transforming a Victorian country house with the addition of a huge range of indoor (and outdoor) leisure pursuits, including swimming pool, squash and other sports facilities, an all-year, all-weather base has been created. Scotland's best equipped time-share lodges—very upmarket—are discreetly hidden in the woodlands, which help make the whole operation viable. Craigendarrach is not cheap, but of its type it is perhaps the UK yardstick, pointing the way forward and showing that modern leisure developments can be discreet and do not have to be 'tacky'.

Ballater can be bypassed, behind the pudding shape of the hill called Craigendarroch immediately north of the town, though only a shortage of time could justify doing so. More relaxed travellers should discover **Glen Muick** (pronounced mick, meaning pig in Gaelic!)—especially if they want to see red deer. To do so, cross the Dee and go right from Ballater, taking a left turn less than a mile further on. The cul-de-sac road soon climbs out of a larch-shaded, white-water valley into a broad glen. Here by the heather and coarse-grass river flats should be deer in plenty. In season, they even prospect around the picnic tables at the car park where the public road ends. Walkers start their excursions from here, perhaps along Loch Muick in the dark hollow further up the glen, or up the Mounth tracks, or to the peak of Lochnagar. This hill's long battlements of snow-fluted cliffs edge the northern skyline—though you will have to walk a long and well-shod way for even a glimpse of its high corrie loch.

The Dee beyond Ballater runs through the pinewoods, rounding granite boulders and pleasing fishermen who can afford the salmon beat prices. The main A93 road continues fast and scenic. A huge car park heralds the nearness of **Balmoral Castle** and is a reminder of the curious enthusiasm of tourists for any kind of Royal association. The whole 'Balmorality' business seemed to spring from the cult of the Picturesque and the Romantic in the late 18C—to which was added a dash of noble savage, that is, post-Culloden tamed Highlander and a queen who built a holiday-home here in the 1850s. The result is an epidemic of unbridled tartanitis, continuing to the present day. As a side effect, an estate on Deeside can still be a goal for fast-buck foreign millionaires. Some of them achieve it.

However, the scenery continues to improve, with more pine-screened glimpses of dark Lochnagar and the much-photographed old bridge at Invercauld (just upstream from where today's bridge crosses the Dee). Soon, you arrive in **BRAEMAR**, though not before noting **Braemar Castle**, a 17C stronghold, altered with star-shaped defences and garrisoned by Hanoverian troops after the 1745 Jacobite rebellion. (The 'Braes of Mar' were the setting for the raising of the Standard in the earlier 1715 rebellion, led by the indecisive Earl of Mar.)

The village of Braemar has a faintly alpine air when the snows fall and has for long been a pausing place for visitors. The River Clunie girns over grey rocks and glowering pools below a bridge near the village centre. It is a reminder that Braemar is within easy range of plenty of scenic spots, but not all of them are accessible to the car-borne traveller! One diversion here is to continue up the valley of the River Dee to the **Linn of Dee**. A linn is a rocky narrowing of waters. Deeside has a number, of which this is perhaps the most spectacular. Take care when taking pictures as the tree-roots are slippy after rain and the waters roar through a deep channel. Afterwards you must retrace your route to Braemar.

Though you may have gone a little way west in the excursion towards the Linn, the main road at Braemar decides against an all-out assault on the Cairngorms and 'slopes off' southwards for Perthshire. Strictly speaking it slopes up Glen Clunie, at least as far as the **Cairnwell Pass**, which at over 2,000ft (620m) is the highest main road in the UK (though not the highest motorable road). The Clunie side is typical Grampian country, with soaring heather-slopes stretching up to high, thin plateau grasslands. At the Cairnwell, the **Glenshee** ski development deeply scars the smooth-flanked uplands, but brings much-needed winter season revenue. Glen Shee rolls down from it and, unless you are a hillwalker on the way to the big dome of the Glas Maol, you will not see the once famous hairpin of the Devil's Elbow. It survives below the wide, straight modern road, on the left, only a mile or so from the summit.

A 'back-road' section now follows as you turn eastwards to continue the circuit of the Mounth. South of the Spittal of Glenshee (strictly speaking Glen Shee starts here and runs south) look for a sign, left, indicating the B951 to Glen Isla and Kirriemuir. This is partly single-track, but wide. It first goes over the open moor, across the watershed and down to the flats (or 'haughs') of the River Isla. Go right just as you see a ruined tower house, to follow the River Isla downstream, through typical upland Grampian scenery: forestry blocks, birches, sheep pasture by the river. There is an attractive picnic site just a little way down the Isla, though there is a 'proper' one, with neatly clipped edging and toilets, a little further at Kirkton of Glenisla.

B951 continues to the Loch of Lintrathen where you become aware of the broad strath opening out southwards as the road begins to turn towards the east to make its way into Strathmore. With the great Grampian shoulders perhaps cloud-hidden on your right, above you, and the cultivated fields below, there is a strong sense of the Highland edge, where upland moor and lowland ploughed ground meet at a field boundary.

Amongst the berry-fields of Strathmore, **KIRRIEMUIR** is noted as the birthplace of J.M. Barrie (1860–1937), novelist, playwright and creator of Peter Pan. The NTS care for **Barrie's Birthplace**, a white cottage with mementoes of Barrie's work. The red sandstone theme, already beginning to predominate in ploughed field tints, adds character to the old town's buildings and winding streets. This market town is gateway to some of the most impressive of the Angus glens, which run deeply into the Mounth from the south.

**Glen Clova** is a classic U-profiled glacial valley with the B955 (signed 'the Glens' from Kirriemuir town centre) giving about 14 miles (22km) of scenic motoring deep into the hills. If you take this diversion, you will find parking places and walks at high or low levels. It is only about 6 miles (10km) as the grouse flies across the high peaty table-land back to the car park in Glen Muick on the Ballater side of the hills. Botanists, with the right contacts, will also find nearby plant sites in the vicinity with some of Britain's rarest flora. Note that the B956 makes a loop part of the way for your return to Dykehead. If coming out of Glen Clova, turn left just before Cortachy to cross the River South Esk on an unclassified road which leads to the key junction of Memus.

If driving from Kirriemuir directly, look for a road called Roods (also signed for camera obscura) on the one-way system just before the post office. This leads up and out of town, past the golf course and into farm-lands with hill views. Disregard a Glen Clova sign, left. Your best route is to stay roughly parallel to the hills, and continue for a few minutes to travel a little north of east till you pick up signs to Memus. Cross the River South Esk and turn left and north, then right and east at the Memus junction. Here you will also find the **Drovers Inn** (030786 322). This is a cosy and friendly place, positively 'English country pub' in its ambience (but none the worse for that, as cheery little country pubs are not really easy to find in Scotland). It serves good-quality sensibly priced lunches and dinners.

A few minutes beyond the junction, go straight on at a crossroads, not left for Glen Ogil. Note the standing stone, another landmark, ahead in the field. This next section, between high hill mass and broad vale, is particularly attractive—not because of dramatic slopes and crags over-whelming the road, but for quite the opposite reason. It is a landscape of open skies and long views hinting of the sea beyond the patterns of fields and trees to the east. The red soils of the Highland edge predominate in spring, a reminder that the soft sandstones were ground down to create the strath—though the ancient Highland rocks to the left proved harder.

Veer left at the hamlet of Tigerton at an unmistakable grey war memorial. The next crossroads is signed (by 'Historic Scotland') left for the **White and Brown Caterthun** forts. These foothill forts are impres-sive examples of an early (perhaps 300BC) community's ability to organise resources to build substantial defences. The White Caterthun makes a short and easy walk from a small car park in the col between the two fortified tops, and, as you climb the last section on foot, a giant panorama-map of the old counties of Angus and Kincardineshire rolls out. The fort itself is a great eerie ring of grey stones, four vague circles of ancient tumbled ramparts.

Retrace your tracks to the car. The road drops off the col ahead of the lonely gloom of high domed hills. Continue to circle north-east and east. Do not go right at Pitmudie Farm, but go right at a T-junction to cross the West Water. After a few minutes you will reach **Edzell Castle**, a russet tower in a green landscape. Shortly before you reach the castle, there is an attractive picnic site, where the road runs just above the tree-lined river. Edzell Castle itself shows the transition between early defen-sive needs and later more peaceable pursuits. It is a 16C fortified tower with a later courtyard house and a 'pleasance'—a walled garden—uniquely overlooked by a variety of heraldic devices and sculptured panels.

Continue to **EDZELL**, a community with a sleepy air along its wide main street. Queen Victoria visited here, arriving under a triumphal stone arch, which still stands at the south end of the town. Go left on to B966, northwards then east to Fettercairn, which also, not to be outdone, built a stone arch for Queen Victoria in 1861. The quickest way back to Aber-deen is to go through this arch and turn right at the roundabout. The top part of the long vale of Strathmore, up which you have been travelling, is known as the Howe (hollow) of the Mearns. B966 continues through the howe, down to the main road (A94) on which you can whizz back to Aberdeen.

However, the Cairn o' Mount road is much more exciting, signed at Fettercairn as B974. This former military road across the Mounth lifts into the hills, past the sometimes overlooked **Fasque** (1809), home of the Gladstones of Prime Ministerial fame. The route rises into grouse-croaking moorland with ever-improving views south over Strathmore and the blue-grey sea, then northwards into the heartlands of Aberdeenshire. Thereafter it drops into woodlands and rolls into the valley of the Water of Feugh and back into the Strathdee farmlands. Go right at Strachan (pronounced something like 'strawn') for Banchory and a choice of roads eastwards for Aberdeen.

## The Buchan Coastline

*1 day/65 miles (104km)/from Aberdeen to Banff*

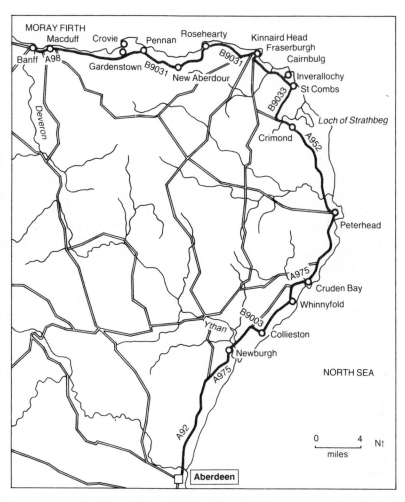

Fareweel to Tarwathie, adieu Mormond Hill
And the dear land of Crimond, I bid thee fareweel,
For we're bound out for Greenland and ready to sail,
In hopes to find riches in hunting the whale.
from the Greig-Duncan Folk Song Collection

*Old Aberdeen*

On their celebrated tour of Scotland, Johnson and Boswell came part of the way up the north-east coastline, then 'cut the corner' north-westwards. Others did the same, as do many of today's road travellers, partly because of the relatively undistinguished, though pleasing enough, countryside of Buchan, the lands nearest the north-east tip. However, in bypassing the arc of land spreading out south-west from the turning-point of Kinnaird Head in Fraserburgh, some of the UK's finest seascapes are missed. This is a route for visitors with a taste for lonely beaches and wild cliffs. The emphasis is on the coastline throughout. Please park sensibly in your explorations, especially in areas of sand-dunes—particularly vulnerable to cutting up by tyre tracks. Most importantly, if you are a dog owner, control your animal on the wilder stretches of dunes and beaches, especially when waders and wildfowl are known to breed in the vicinity.

**ABERDEEN** pop. 191,000 Tourist Information Centre: St Nicholas House, Broad Street (0224 632727/637353). Unique among British cities for its emphasis on locally quarried granite as a building material. Aberdeen's main shopping street, Union Street, not yet overwhelmed by faceless modern shopping developments, still has many fine Victorian buildings which use this silvery-grey material in great confident blocks. (The older suburbs also make fascinating touring.) However, this tough and unyielding rock's finest use is in **Marischal College**, a spired and sparkling façade decorating the second-largest granite building in the world. **Art Gallery**, **Maritime Museum**, 16C **Provost Skene's House**, the wonderfully ornate **His Majesty's Theatre** are just a few of the city's attractions. Aberdeen also prides itself on its floral displays, softening the hard-edged granite. It wins Britain in Bloom competitions with such regularity that it is often banned from entering them! A spring or high summer visit here reveals a wealth of colour escaping out of parks into every public space—even the ring-road's central reservation is like a linear rose catalogue.

Though it would be equally appropriate to leave Aberdeen by the harbour and promenade to catch the maritime flavour of this route right at the start, this northward journey is convenient for taking in **Old Aberdeen** and **King's College**. Formerly an independent burgh clustered round its university, Old Aberdeen still retains a peaceful academic air around its main street of College Bounds (parallel to King Street, your way north).

The centrepiece is the crown spire of **King's College Chapel** (1500). Inside the building is Scotland's finest surviving medieval woodworking.

Northwards, College Bounds ends with the handsome **Town House** (1788), beyond which the Chanonry leads to **St Machar's Cathedral**, built and rebuilt from 1370 onwards and marrying red sandstone and silver granite. You must return to King Street to go left (signposted) for a view of the venerable **Brig o' Balgownie**, north of Seaton Park. Built 1314–18, this bridge was the only crossing point to the north until 1827.

Set course on the A92, at first a dual carriageway. Sandy beaches run for about 10 miles (16km) from Aberdeen north via Balmedie (now with housing estates, typical of the oil-boom north-east, and a country park) to the village of **NEWBURGH**, which you reach by going right via the A975. Coastal exploration can start beyond the road bridge that spans the Ythan (pronounced '*eye*-than'). There is a small car park for the **Sands of Forvie**. The Nature Conservancy Council care for the fascinating landscapes on the north side of the river—a complex which starts with humps of wind-carved dunes by the river mouth, northwards fixed by marram grass, and in turn giving rise to sandy heath and rough heather. Birdwatchers will have the odd experience of hearing eider duck make their distinct crooning, while in the background red grouse cackle—a most unusual combination of habitat. Parts of the reserve, which contains Britain's highest breeding population of eider duck, are fenced off, quite rightly, in the breeding season. The **Foveran House Hotel** (03586 89398) screened and sheltered by a tree-lined drive, makes a relaxed country-house style lunch-stop (at least).

The sandy strip becomes rocky near **COLLIESTON** which is reached by B9003, signed right, barely 2 miles (3km) above the Ythan Bridge. This road reaches the former fishing settlement round the top edge of the Sands of Forvie. Huddled round a rocky crescent, Collieston was once famous for its 'speldings'—split and dried haddocks. At the entrance to the village an unclassified road is signed Whinnyfold. This road wends its way among featureless hillocks for a short distance, past a fragment, glimpsed down by the shore, of Old Slains Castle, destroyed by James VI in 1594. Views improve with the Bay of Cruden emerging ahead with the dark shape of 'new' Slains Castle at its far end seen dimly through the haze of breakers. A sign points the way right down to **WHINNYFOLD**, just a few rows of cottages overlooking a small stony bay, a habitation which could not be closer to the elements of rock, wind and wild water.

Beyond the craggy shores, the perfect sand curves round to the more substantial village of **CRUDEN BAY**, a community with a little harbour and the main access by footbridge to the beach. The name may mean 'Croju-Dane', slaughter of the Danes, recalling an ancient battle and the Scandinavian links along this coast. Both to north and south are caves associated with smuggling—a very popular activity in former times. Cruden Bay's golf course has a high reputation and played its part in an early tourism venture. Noting the success of the Glasgow and South-Western Railway's Turnberry Hotel and the Gleneagles of the Caledonian Railway, the Great North of Scotland Railway built a grand red-granite hotel here, hoping this brisk and bracing coastline would become a popular resort. It was a failure: railway, connecting tramway and the hotel itself have vanished. (The building survived until 1950.)

Strictly speaking the harbour here is called Port Erroll, recalling the Earls of Erroll, the local landowners who formerly lived at **Slains Castle**. Said to have been the setting which inspired Bram Stoker's *Dracula*, this straggling roofless ruin on the clifftop is reached by a poorly surfaced road north of Cruden Bay. (At time of writing, the castle had been bought by developers.) James Boswell, fawning and flattering his way round Scotland, and round Dr Samuel Johnson, arrived with his hero at precisely 3pm on Tuesday 24 August 1773. They were well entertained by the Boyd family who ensured they saw the local wonder, the **Bullers of Buchan**, the most dramatic spot on a coastline of cliffs and sea-foam.

This fearsome place is another mile to the north, signed off the A975, which you have now rejoined. For long a tourist curiosity, it even had its own station on the nearby (closed) Ellon-Boddam branch-line. Its visitors come to peer deep into a kind of roofless sea cave or arch, a black pot echoing to the cackles of fulmars. Not for the unsteady footed. Doctor Johnson described the rock as 'perpendicularly tubulated', though you may not notice.

Granite outcrops on the coast northwards, with more dramatic seascapes, though the hinterland continues spare and open. To reach **PETERHEAD** go right at the A975 junction with the A952 along a far-from-scenic section past Peterhead power station. The route also runs by the old fishing community of Boddam with its lighthouse on a rocky islet, tethered to the mainland by a narrow bridge. Peterhead's locally quarried granite was used in the construction of the town's harbour of refuge, built with convict labour from its infamous prison. The town today is a busy, down-to-earth, not overly picturesque place, its older properties showing its characteristic local pinkish granite. It once had an active whale fishery, recalled in the town's **Arbuthnott Museum**.

Peterhead has played its part in the oil industry, partly because of the shelter of the breakwaters in the bay, and also developed its harbour into the largest white-fish landing port in Europe. The impressive size of some of the vessels to be seen when the fleet is in port, not to mention the up-market badging of the cars on the quayside, indicates a perilous prosperity, a phenomenon repeated further round the coast at Fraserburgh, Macduff and beyond.

Leaving the town northwards on A952, note the **Waterside Inn**

*The Bullers of Buchan*

110

(0779 71121), a large modern hotel offering good value, given its range of facilities. As you make your way north, you look half-left into the heart of the Buchan landscape, around the low humps of Mormond Hill. Apart from the hill's ever-diminishing moorlands, nearly all around is the 'landscape of improvement', the dry-stane dykes (walls hereabouts) a reminder of lifetimes of toil to break in the fields. Too austere to be conventionally attractive, these spare farmscapes are the very essence of Buchan's cold shoulders.

Past the British Gas Terminal at St Fergus, scarcely tucked behind its green screening ramparts, A952 gives access to a remote sandy coastline at a number of places. Separated from the sea only by a spit of empty dunes is the important RSPB reserve of the **Loch of Strathbeg**, a vital wintering ground and migration staging post for vast numbers of wildfowl. Continue on the main road to look for the kirk clock with six minutes between 11 and 12 o'clock at Crimond, whose name is also recalled in the 23rd Psalm tune, written by a daughter of the manse. Within a mile or two beyond, go right at crossroads, signed St Combs (B9033).

The villages of **ST COMBS, INVERALLOCHY** and **CAIRNBULG** are close communities of mainly fisher families. Once the boats were hauled out on to the beaches, as in so many other north-east coastal settlements. Now the crews work out of Fraserburgh or Peterhead, though their vessels still have the village names painted on them. Gable-ends to the sea, these 'fishertouns' are the very core of coastal Buchan, with language, traditions and a sense of belonging still unshaken by the obvious trappings of modernity.

Return to B9033 and head north for Fraserburgh, noting as you cross the Waters of Philorth (pronounce 'florth'), left, Cairnbulg Castle and right, the bridge-piers of the light railway (Fraserburgh–St Combs, closed 1965) whose locomotives were fitted with cow-catchers, American-style, because of the unfenced line. There is access to Fraserburgh beach here as well, and wild orchids amongst the dunes, if you know where to look, and if the locals' cars haven't parked on them.

**FRASERBURGH**, locally called 'the Broch', is grey and graceless at first sight, but is only going about its business, much of it tied up with fishing. Fall into conversation with the local folk and you will find them friendly and ready to direct you to the lighthouse, the lifeboat shed or their beach which has won the EEC's Blue Flag award—though not consistently—for cleanliness (one of the few in the UK). The lighthouse, right at the north-east tip—Kinnaird Head, the *Promontorium taixalium* of Roman maps—was the first to be built in Scotland by the Northern Lighthouse Trustees in 1787. It sits, uniquely, on top of the former castle seat of the Frasers, the town's founding family.

West of the town, take B9031 which hugs an undistinguished shore (unless you are a curlew, in which case it has five stars). Somewhere on this unfrequented strand a curious incident took place in 1556 with which even Queen Mary of England became involved. An English ship, the *Edward Bonaventure*, carrying the first ever Russian ambassador to the English Court, was wrecked here, along with its cargo of furs and jewels.

The ambassador was saved, although the news took 26 days to reach London, but the quick-witted locals made sure the precious cargo was never seen again! Queen Mary even obtained permission from Scotland for troops to search the area to no avail.

The sea-gabled, single-storeyed houses of **Sandhaven**, with its broken-down harbour but still active boat-building yard, set the theme for the way west along a gradually rising coast which eventually towers into cliff scenery the equal in spectacle to anywhere on the British mainland. Follow B9031 through **ROSEHEARTY**, eclipsed by Fraserburgh as a fishing port after the railway arrived (good picnic places along the coast west from here). Note above the village the 15C ruins of **Pitsligo Castle**. (Restoration is likely.) This was formerly the seat of the Forbes family. Alexander Forbes the fourth and last Lord Pitsligo, like many other north-east families, was an active Jacobite and had a price on his head after the 1745 rebellion. His people never betrayed him, though for some time after he went about the countryside disguised as a beggar. Maps mark a Lord Pitsligo's Cave west of Rosehearty.

Continue to New Aberdour by the B9031. (There is a little road nearer the coast, giving good cliff views, but it is narrow and not recommended.)

**NEW ABERDOUR** conforms to the pattern of many planned settlements in the north-east. It was laid out in 1798 and replaced an inconveniently sited 'kirktoun' which you will see if you continue on B9031, signed Gardenstown, and then take the narrow road down the valley of the Dour Burn. Old Aberdour kirk was founded, it is said, by St Columba himself and dedicated to his nephew St Drostan. Beyond the kirkyard, the little road gives access to a pebble beach with red sandstone caved cliffs. In rough weather, the pebbles rub and roar with each receding wave, like applause from a huge audience.

Retrace your route a short way then continue on B9031, tricky in this next section as it hairpins and blind-bends its way west. Watch the road signs carefully, as they do not exaggerate the short but steep gradients. Soon you reach the crossroads for **PENNAN**, a single crescent of white houses tucked well into the cliff-base and reached by a sharply tilted road. The **Pennan Inn** (03466 201), like the rest of the village, gained a transient fame for its role in the film *Local Hero*, though the sand-scenes were shot at Morar near Mallaig, miles away on the west coast.

At the top of the hill again, the road goes on to Cullykhan Bay, a tiny sand-strip with the rocky drama of Hell's Lum and the Lion's Head nearby. Both sides of Pennan have cliffs around the 350ft (106m) mark and the road soars out of Cullykhan taking an inland course across the rough fields. The first signpost for **GARDENSTOWN** also takes the motorist to a car park above the extraordinary settlement of **CROVIE**, which looks like a line of houses humped seal-like out of the sea to lie basking above high water. Until recent years there was only a shoreline path from Crovie to Gardenstown.

Return to B9031 to bypass Gardenstown as the best view of the two settlements is from a rough road to the west of the village, which leaves the main road at a tight right-hand bend. There is a small car park, beyond which a short walk brings you to the roofless kirk of St John, founded by the locals in 1004 in thanksgiving for their defeat of Norse raiders. Set on a steeply tilting green slope, the kirk offers a wide view back east towards Gardenstown, its colonies of houses festooned across the steep face which leads down to its harbour. Almost invariably called Gamrie, this tightly-knit community is noted as a stronghold of evangelical faiths.

Between Gardenstown and the junction with the main A98, there is more of a sense of the rolling Buchan landscape chopped off short, just a few fields away to the north, than an actual sight of the great grassy tiers and cliffs which career into the sea on this spectacular coast. Turn right on the A98 for Macduff and Banff. If the weather is clear over the firth, you will see the hills of Caithness, faint and smudgy to the north-west.

**MACDUFF**, though smaller than Fraserburgh or Peterhead, is the third of the north-east fishing ports on this stretch of coast. The **Highland Haven** (0261 32408) has a restaurant overlooking the harbour. Traditional boatbuilding survives at the port.

Macduff's older neighbour **BANFF** is moments away and separated only by the combed-back waves rolling up the estuary of the River Deveron. After the austere granite of so much of the local architecture, Banff's elegant Georgian town houses are a surprise. The imposing William Adam-designed Duff House stands in parkland nearby, but the chief delight is the wealth of restored domestic 17–19C architecture, as a walk along High Street and High Shore will reveal. In the town centre, the grouping of mercat cross, town house and tolbooth steeple, ancient symbols of commercial life, is a reminder that Banff was made a Royal Burgh before the end of the 12C.

Though Banff is the end of this excursion, it is also a gateway to the delights of the rural and sheltered inner Moray Firth touched by routes 'North-East Castles and Coastline' (below) and, more extensively, 'The Inner Moray Firth' (p. 124).

# North-East Castles and Coastline

*2–4 days/145 miles (232km)/from the Kildrummy or Alford area*

> *O gin I were whaur the Gadie rins,*
> *At the back o Bennachie.*

> Traditional

Many an exile wishes to return to the lands around the Gadie Burn in the hinterland of Aberdeenshire, within sight of the hill of Bennachie, which overlooks the well-kept farmlands on one side and the higher Grampians to the west. The farmers of the old counties of Aberdeen, Banff and Moray have done battle for centuries with the moors of the Grampian

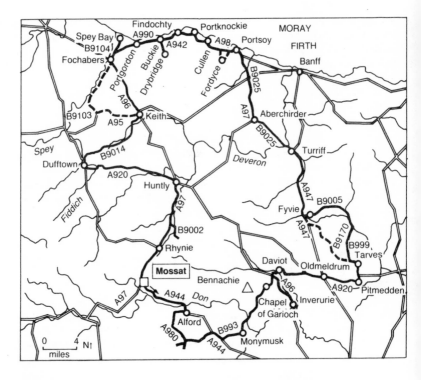

hills, which send their outliers towards the sea. On the eastern portion of this route, around Pitmedden, for instance, the high ground has dropped back westward, with only the guardian hill of Bennachie easily visible. But further west, beyond Huntly, the uplands rise out of a falling tide of field and forest. But both the low ground 'parks' and the Grampian edge share the same feature of a wealth of castles.

This route has a number of equally good starting points: at opposite ends, for example, both Elgin and Aberdeen lie within easy reach. It can also be reached from the west or south coming in from A97 at the Mossat junction. Thus the starting point described below is of a more arbitrary nature than any other in this book. Also, note that the erratic path north-west of Huntly is given as a much pleasanter alternative to the downright dangerous A96.

You could start by making your way off A944 between Mossat and Alford to visit **Kildrummy Castle** on A97. This magnificently ruined medieval fortress—the most extensive remains of any 13C castle in Scotland—played an important role in Scotland's history. Its final drama before it was dismantled was as the Earl of Mar's headquarters during the 1715 Jacobite rebellion. The curious shield-shaped fortress, said to be modelled on the Château de Coucy at Laon, was designed by St Gilbert, the last of the Scottish saints. Behind it, laid out in the quarry from which the castle stonework was won, are **Kildrummy Castle Gardens**, a springtime delight with rare alpines, glowing azaleas and the great yellow spathes of the American skunk cabbage poking boldly out of the waterside. **Kildrummy Castle Hotel** (09756 71288) is on the edge of the garden and overlooks the castle. This grand mansion offers very high standards of accommodation and cuisine.

Return to the junction at Mossat, where the local shop on the left offers a good cup of tea, and turn right, on to A944 for **ALFORD**. This is a pleasantly wooded drive by the River Don. Alford is a quietly attractive village with the **Grampian Museum of Transport** as one of its attractions. This mainly road vehicle orientated museum includes such local machines as the 'Craigievar Express' a steam-driven cart built by the local postman! Railway enthusiasts have a separate little museum in what was once the station at this long-vanished branch-line. A miniature railway, much enjoyed by children, now links the site with Haughton Park.

On any section of road in what is called for administrative purposes Gordon District (though it will always be Aberdeenshire for the natives) you will see signs for the Castle Trail, the heavily promoted tour of the best of Gordon's castles. This route dips in and out of the trail and the signs will help you find **Craigievar Castle** off A980, south of Alford. Craigievar is often described as the finest of the Grampian castles, a pink-harled (rough-cast) confection standing in the woods and farmlands, much as the builders of 1626 left it. Occupied continuously by the Forbes or Forbes Semphill families until its presentation to the NTS in 1963, this mostly accounts for its unaltered condition. Inside there is a high standard of craftsmanship in decorative plasterwork and carved panelling, all commissioned by its original owner, William Forbes—'Willie the Marchant of Aberdeen'.

*Craigievar Castle*

You could return to Alford to continue east, but after Craigievar go left at the road-end and you will soon see a sign for Touch (pronounced 'tooch' with a Scots 'ch') on your right as you go north. This narrow little road takes you deep into the farming hinterland. Views open out over your beacon and landmark, the hill of Bennachie, and Donside northwards, while white stars of wood anemones drift below the trees in the foreground. You then rejoin A944. Go right and shortly left on B993 signed Castle Fraser. Do visit this castle if time permits—dated 1575–1636, it is in the forefront of the great native flowering of 16/17C castle building, from which masterpieces like Craigievar or Crathes (p. 102) sprang. However, our route turns off within 3 miles (5km), at **MONYMUSK**.

The earliest settlement here, a religious community of Irish origin, predates by several centuries the late 12C or early 13C **St Mary's Church** (behind the main square) which itself incorporates features of the place of worship of a 12C Augustinian settlement. The chancel arch is Norman, and the interior also features good modern stained glass and a Pictish symbol stone. You may have to content yourself, however, with the information panel on a nearby wall, as the church is not always open. The helpful panel also describes the symmetrical style of the planned village built by the great improving laird, Sir Archibald Grant of Monymusk, who initiated a scheme to plant 50 million trees on the Monymusk estates.

For a closer look at the policies, as well as Bennachie, you must follow Chapel of Garioch signs out of the village, though you should note that the **Lord's Throat** is also signed and makes a worthwhile diversion, left again up the river valley of the Don by dense woodlands with walking trails. If you investigate this short section, return to the Chapel of Garioch road and continue northwards where impressive views of **Bennachie** (1,733ft/537m), close at hand, open up. Around the evocative granite tor, the tumbled walls of a fort of perhaps the first century AD can be made out. As you drive this route, you can speculate whether or not this hill really is the Mons Graupius mentioned by the Roman historian Tacitus. He tells how, in the summer of AD83, Agricola's wide-ranging forces finally brought to battle a large group of Caledonian warriors and defeated them on a hillslope just within sight of the sea in the very far north of Scotland. Speculation that this was the site increased after the discovery of a Roman temporary or marching camp at nearby Durno in 1977. (Incidentally, Tacitus's history was printed in the 1470s with the printing error of an 'm' for a 'u' and hence Grampian which ought to be Graupian!)

At the Chapel of Garioch crossroads go left for more evidence of the early folk of the north. A short way down, the **Maiden Stone**, a pink granite monolith carved with Pictish beasts, is conspicuous on your left by the roadside—park at a layby a little further on and walk back. The 'elephant' and the mirror and comb stand out best in strong sideways light, say around midday in the early months of the year. The work is very late—around the 9C AD. Return to Chapel of Garioch to take a left beyond the village (signed Pitcaple) to bring you to the main A96.

You have a choice here. You could take in **INVERURIE**, right, on A96—good shopping, local museum—or continue a peaceful rural drive by heading across country by back-roads. If you decide to pursue the rural theme, then go right (take care crossing the busy A96), then left almost immediately, signed Whiteford and Durno. Within a few hundred yards, go right, signed Oldmeldrum, then, as a final test of your navigational skills, look for a sign left, by a quarry, for **DAVIOT**. This is actually easier to drive than to describe!

Even if you miss the Daviot sign, there are later left turns to take you there. This little dormitory community, which you will see ahead of you on a broad rise, is included because of the views from its nearby stone circle, which lies just beyond Daviot at its far or north end. The **Loanhead Stone Circle** is a place to let your imagination take wing. Within the recumbent stones is a now-depleted great ring cairn. To one side is a later and much less substantial or significant cremation cemetery, set within arcs of low stone walling. Archaeologists think the site was used for several centuries, and was abandoned about 2000BC. Yet there may be a link with the present. Some say part of the function of these great stone rings was to measure the seasons, to calculate the best time for sowing. Take a look to the north-east, beyond the boundary fence. The landscape you see, with its neat fields and the far-off clanking of a tractor, is completely man-made, through the efforts of perhaps the direct descendants of those shadowy folk, who had the same preoccupation with the seasons.

As you return to the car through a pleasant swathe of woodland, Bennachie still spreads across the westward view. In the other direction, you should also have spotted the little community of Oldmeldrum from Loanhead and you can set a course for it by sight, dropping down from Daviot by going left immediately after the right-angled turn in the village. **OLDMELDRUM** is old-established and not numbered among the north-east's planned villages. The curving, irregular street layout around a characterful and now conserved town-centre recalls its medieval origins. It was a former Burgh of Barony (a step below a Royal Burgh) only over-taken by Inverurie as a local centre in the 19C. The **Glengarioch Distillery** here produces not only a single malt whisky, but also tomatoes and pot plants in its greenhouses using waste heat from the condensers. In the village centre, the **Meldrum Arms** (06512 2238/2505) offers 'middle of the road' good value accommodation (and bar meals), while the **Meldrum House Hotel** (06512 2294), signed off A947 north, is in the big league of country house experiences—13C, 1,500-acre estate— with a long-established reputation for its cuisine and accommodation standards.

Head east on A947 (A920) with the Castle Trail signed. Take A920 for Pitmedden and Tolquhon, pronounced 'tu*hoon*'. By this time you will notice that the landscape interest has been left westwards. Though pleasant enough, this is serious farming country with business-like grey-roofed farms and stables growing out of the well-cropped parks—which is what fields are called in the north-east.

The interest hereabouts focuses instead on the fine properties. NTS signs will bring you in to **PITMEDDEN** first, via B999. **Pitmedden Garden and Museum of Farming Life**, almost unique in Scotland, is a recreation by the NTS of a 17C garden, originally laid out by Sir Alexander Seaton, with intricate floral patterns, pavilions and fountains. It is at its best in high summer when the thousands of bedding plants have picked out the designs within the clipped box-edging.

Stay on B999 to reach **Tolquhon**, signed left. Once a Forbes family seat, this ruin is an early 15C rectangular tower with a slightly later mansion attached. There are two towers, carved panels and a courtyard. After the roofed splendours of the other castles on the way, you may have to exercise your imagination here. The roofless property is in the care of Historic Scotland, that is, in the case of the government body responsible for historic properties. (You can usually easily tell an NTS from an HS property. The NTS prefers its stately homes with roofs on!)

The next NTS property is a short way to the north, signed right off B999, before the village of Tarves. **Haddo House** is approached by a long drive across the estate's fields and plantations, some of them created by the improving Fourth Earl of Aberdeen (UK Prime Minister during the Crimean War). By now you may be in need of the tea-room, which is thankfully close to the car park, before you have even examined the magnificent winged frontage of the mansion. The Second Earl, William Gordon, commissioned William Adam to design a grand new house. Though there was some later alteration, the idea of integrating house and landscape can still be appreciated. There is plenty of interest inside and out, the sense of restrained luxury enhanced by the occasional burst of harp music from the library, as the NTS adds further atmosphere in high season.

The road to Fyvie Castle is now signed on a circular route by B9170/B9005 via Methlick. Bolder navigators can strike across country via Barthol Chapel to join A947. Either way, the rambling pile of **Fyvie Castle** is signed from the village of Fyvie. After the lightness and elegance of Haddo, you may find Fyvie positively rambling and oppressive, a plausible setting for the chilling tale or two with which the place is associated. Inside, inspect the scale model of the castle first, if you wish to make sense of the great towers added by the successive families of Preston, Meldrum, Seton and Gordon who rebuilt the original quadrangular 13C fortress over the centuries. In 1899 it finally came into the hands of returning local man Alexander Forbes-Leith, who had made his fortune in the USA. He fitted it out with sumptuous Edwardian interiors and filled it with fine paintings, including more than a dozen Raeburns. If after this rich diet you can still take more opulence, then the local kirk in **FYVIE** may be lost in the heart of rural Aberdeenshire, but boasts two magnificent Tiffany windows, gifted by the Forbes-Leiths.

Make your way to **TURRIFF**, called Turra locally, on A947. This pleasing red-sandstone market-centre in the rural hinterland was in ancient times a centre for the Knights Templar. Even earlier, in the 7C, one of the north-east's first churches was founded here. The ruins of Turriff's 11C Auld Kirk, with a belfry of 1636, lie west of the mercat cross in today's town. Around this cross were formerly held the great 'feein mercats' or hiring fairs for farm servants. Even today, Turriff still has a thriving livestock mart twice weekly.

To an older generation of local farming folk, the town is recalled in the locally well-known incident of the 'Turra Coo': in 1913 a local farmer refused to participate in a newly introduced National Health Insurance Scheme. Legal proceedings followed, with one of his cows seized to be publicly auctioned in Turriff in lieu of a fine. A thousand protesters gathered and pelted the sheriff's officers with eggs and rotting cabbages. The cow bolted, but was eventually sold at Aberdeen, whereupon local farmers bought it back. They presented it with great ceremony to its original owner—now a local hero for his stand against authority—watched by 2,000 spectators and the Turriff brass band! North-east folk are perhaps thrawn (stubborn), but at least show independence of thought and spirit.

Take B9025, signed Aberchirder—pronounced locally 'Foggieloan'—then join A97, turning right. Exit left for **PORTSOY**, exchanging the green fields of Banffshire for coastal breezes. Portsoy is an attractive little community with a period flavour thanks to an enlightened policy of building renewal particularly around the harbour, which is said to be one of the oldest (1692) on the Moray Firth. It developed very early trade links with Europe, then played its part in the 19C herring-boom, but the little port is now used mainly by pleasure craft. Portsoy is also associated with a type of marble or serpentine, which polishes well and was even used in the Palace of Versailles in France. Nowadays, it is made into decorative brooches and giftwares in a harbourside workshop open to visitors.

Take the main A98 west of Portsoy. You can divert left on a minor road signed for **FORDYCE** to view this charming conservation village with its vaguely 'English village green' ambience, somewhat unexpected amongst the rolling barleyfields of Banffshire. You then return to the main road at Sandend Bay and can divert again, right this time for the little community of **Sandend**, set by the side of a pale and inviting shore.

However, for an even better beach, leave Sandend by a little road going west, opposite the caravan site. Within a mile, look for a sign to Sunnyside Beach. Park in the farmyard, as advised by a sign and walk the short way down to a rocky shore. Perched on a headland below the green edge you will see the ruined **Findlater Castle**. A 15C seat of the Ogilvies, the exposed and windswept site was abandoned in the mid-17C for the more comfortable and ornate Cullen House. A little further west the low grassy cliffs give way to a glittering strip of rock-bound sand—no ice-cream vans, no facilities of any kind. Perhaps, in the quiet season, no people.

Return to the main road by turning right at the farm road-end. Following the minor road through a right angle takes you to A98. Turn right for **CULLEN**. This is one of the most attractive of the Moray Firth resorts, neatly laid out from 1821 onwards on the instructions of the Earl of Seafield who lived at nearby Cullen House. He considered the old village too close and demolished it. The focus of the community is the main square, which tilts seawards, with a fine view down the well-proportioned main street and through a handsome railway viaduct to the blue waters and the separate old fishertoun by the shore. The power of the local lairds is demonstrated again: the costly viaduct of the now vanished railway was only necessary because the Earl of Seafield refused the Great North of

Scotland Railway Company permission to build on his land.

The former coaching inn, the **Seafield Arms Hotel** (0542 40791), gives friendly service if you call for a pub lunch, though the **Bayview Hotel and Restaurant** (0542 40432) overlooking the harbour likewise has a very good local reputation and specialises in seafood. Also of interest in Cullen is the late medieval **St Mary's Collegiate Church**—the Auld Kirk—with its armorial panels and ornate tombs as well as the 'laird's loft' of the unavoidable Ogilvie Earls of Seafield.

Leave Cullen by A98, taking care on the bend below the viaduct arches, and at the top of the hill take A942 right for **PORTKNOCKIE**. This old fishing settlement on the cliffs overlooking its tiny harbour shows the typical pattern of well-scrubbed fisher houses, with positively gleaming paintwork, seemingly an essential requirement in all of these communities. Just east of the town and viewed from a wildflower-carpeted clifftop, is the strangely shaped Bow-Fiddle Rock.

Follow A942 westwards towards **FINDOCHTY**, another variation on the brightly themed fishing communities. This time the flavour is almost Mediterranean, with colourful houses ranged round a pleasure-craft-filled harbour. The locals pronounce the place 'Fin*nech*ty' with the appropriate 'ch' sound. Continuing westwards, you soon drop to shore level and reach a string of fishing communities—Portessie, Lanstown, Gordonsburgh—standing gable-end to the sea below low green cliffs on the way to the main port of Buckie. Net-drying greens, sharp-fanged rocks and the blue hills of Caithness across the Firth make for some interesting photo compositions.

**BUCKIE** is a major fishing port, a grey-roofed workaday town, the result of the north-eastern trend towards larger harbours from the smaller communities and, like the others, sharing a prosperity made uncertain by EEC fishing quota restrictions. Its older fisher houses, with the original net stores in the loft area now mainly converted, and the varied churches reflecting a range of religious sects, are typical of north-east fishing communities. The **Maritime Museum and Peter Anson Gallery** continues the fishing theme.

A942 returns to the main A98 from Buckie. An excellent restaurant lies to the south of the town. Take A942, cross A98 to join a minor road signed Drybridge and follow the road uphill and into trees till you see the **Old Monastery** (0542 32660) on your left. As its name suggests, this is a former religious establishment, though only founded in Victorian times. You can enjoy dinner in the chapel and the Moray coast must be the place for fresh seafood.

*Bow-Fiddle Rock*

As an alternative you can continue west of Buckie on A990, taking a minor road at Portgordon then turning right on B9104 for the open reaches of **Spey Bay** and **Tugnet**. The River Spey slows in its speedy course to meet the sea behind a grey and creamy-stoned beach—a long storm-bar of designer door-stops and patio decorations. (Please do *not* take any of these stones home as they sulk and go dull!) Just by the car park is **Tugnet Ice House** telling the story of the Spey. The ice house—dated 1830 and probably the largest in Scotland—is quite literally named. Before its present role as an interpretative centre, it was used by the commercial salmon fishery for preserving the catches. There is also an information board on the start of the official long-distance footpath the **Speyside Way** which sets out upstream from here on its journey to Tomintoul.

Return by B9104 and turn left on A96 for **FOCHABERS**. The Fourth Duke of Gordon, of the rich, local land-owning Gordon family, laid out the village, moving it from its original site by the castle to be out of sight from the family seat. (Gordon Castle is private.) You have already met this common enough whim of the rich and powerful at Cullen. The village's conservation status has helped preserve the building styles of 200 years ago. Today, Fochabers could be a peaceful place, except for the A96 which rattles through the main street. It has a wide range of attractions for a comparatively small community, including an excellent plant nursery, **Christies**, just beyond the A96/A98 junction and **Fochabers Folk Museum**, an entertaining local museum which you enter through one of the town's numerous antique shops. Across the river to the west is the major attraction of **Baxters of Speyside Visitor Centre**. This major quality food producing company, still locally owned and independent, is well equipped for visitors and very popular both with local day-trippers and international visitors. The company offers factory tours, a company museum and period shop—a rebuild of the Baxters' first in Fochabers—as well as an audio/visual show and a Victorian Kitchen tearoom and giftshop.

Though the A96 here can take you south, an option is available, but only for leisurely drivers. It includes a short section on what might be the narrowest road in this book! If coming from the west or River Spey side of the town, turn right into East Street, opposite the converted church housing the local museum. Simply follow this little road out of the houses and into pleasant country lanes. A Forestry Commission sign directs you to the **Earth Pillars**. Follow a path crunchy with pine cones to see these odd formations in the foreground of views beyond a steep, tree-clad slope, which overlooks the River Spey and the farmlands of Moray.

Continue on this narrow road through dense woodland with one spectacular hairpin across a stream-valley, then take a left turn soon after to arrive on B9103, which is then followed east, left again, for Mulben, going straight on to the A95. This brings you to **KEITH**, a busy market centre and gateway to the area's own Whisky Trail to the south-west. The older parts of the town are seen first, closer to the river, while the grid of streets, especially the main shopping street with the square at its far end, suggest that this is yet another planned town, this time by the Second Earl of Seafield in 1750. In the town the **Strathisla Distillery**, built in 1786 on a pleasingly small scale, claims to be the oldest established in Scotland—though other places claim likewise! It has a reception centre with a video presentation. Finally, though the town has several other points of interest, one quaintly offbeat point to note is that a certain (James) Gordon Bennett, born near Keith, was one of many Scots who emigrated to the New World. He founded the *New York Herald* and is one of the few people to be recalled in an English expletive.

To avoid the A96, take B9014 out of Keith, signed Dufftown. A few minutes from the town the **Mill of Towie** is signed. Here, the virtues of 'oat cuisine' can be discovered. Oats, the Scots traditional food, are ground on the premises of this restored mill as in former times. The miller gives tours and there is a restaurant. The road then continues pleasantly to **DUFFTOWN**. Just under the railway bridge, you cross the River Fiddich. If the name sounds familiar, then you will not be surprised to find the **Glenfiddich Distillery**, steaming gently nearby—go right just over the bridge. This distillery, still privately owned, set the pattern for other distilleries to follow by opening its doors to the public in 1969. Its audio/visual programme is evocative, its tour-guides knowledgeable and entertaining. The tours themselves seem to feature a different smell in each department—from the moist, yeasty scents in the huge pine washbacks to the heady spirit reek down the line from the polished copper stills. Glenfiddich, most unusually, also bottles on the premises. You may find the bottling plant hypnotic. The visitor centre portrays the full history of the company.

Note just before the works, above and on the left, half-hidden by trees, the foursquare outline of **Balvenie Castle**, a ruined stronghold whose distinguished visitors included King Edward I of England in 1302 and Mary Queen of Scots in 1562. After the castle, turn left at the road junction by the distillery, and circle into uptown Dufftown, much of it the creation of the Fourth Earl of Fife, James Duff, in 1817. If you turn left again by the handsome clock tower, the little town's focal point (and where you will find the local-interest summer-only museum), you can drop down to a sign, turning sharply right for **Mortlach Church**. This is one of the oldest of Scotland's religious sites, said to have been founded in 566 by a contemporary of St Columba. Though the building was reconstructed in 1876 and 1931 there are many fragments from earlier times: Pictish stones in the vestibule, a lepers' squint in the north wall, three 13C windows in the chancel. Note that the watch-house, built to guard against body-snatchers, now houses the central heating!

Returning from the kirk to the main road, go right and right again at the junction to pick up the A920 for Huntly. There is an atmospheric, ruined castle nearby, to which it may be worth taking a short diversion. **Auchindoun Castle** can be seen, or visited, by going a short way down the A941 road, signed right, for Rhynie. At time of writing, the farm track which leads in under a mile to the castle, was poorly signposted.

Surrounded by prehistoric earthworks, the gaunt and eyeless 15C tower stands against the skyline on a bluff above the River Fiddich. Return to the road junction, going right for Huntly.

You glimpse Auchindoun again behind and to your right as you take the Huntly road, which then gradually drops out of rounded hill, moor and rough pasture for the lowlands by the River Deveron. Go right, briefly on to the A96 to reach the town.

**HUNTLY** stands on an old-established site of strategic importance, guarding the routes northwards from Aberdeen and Strathdon into Moray. It became the power-base of the influential Gordon clan and was—like so many other places in the north-east—expanded and laid out anew (by a later Duke of Gordon). In its rural hinterland it is an important market centre with a weekly livestock mart.

The ruined former Gordon stronghold of **Huntly Castle** is at the far end of the town, beyond the main square. Go through the Gordon Schools' archway and down towards the river to find the great ruined pile topping a 12C motte and bailey. The defensive structures built in succession here became in their final form an ornate palace built around the beginning of the 17C. Though roofless and empty, the building is still impressive, with outstanding decorative work on the oriel windows—inspired by the French Château Blois—fine fireplaces and what have been rated as the most elaborate heraldic adornments to be seen in Scotland.

Take the A97 southwards from the town and up Strathbogie, amongst the farmlands of the River Bogie on its way to meet the Deveron by Huntly Castle. **Leith Hall** is signed left, down B9002. This mansion house—not at all fortress-like, you may by now note with relief as you approach down the long drive—is in the care of the NTS. It offers an insight into the workings of what would in these parts be called 'the big hoose' that is, the local grand property with its estate and tenant farmers, domestic staff and role in local life. In addition to its fine interiors, there is also a pleasant garden and a selection of walks and trails.

South from Leith Hall, a minor road goes to **Clatt**, a blink of a village, but worth seeking out for the **Village Hall** country teas and shop. This community-run enterprise has helped put the little place back on the map. It is said folk travel for miles for the home-made cream meringues alone. Return to the A97 to continue south, with the hillfort-topped **Tap o' Noth** behind, where a rim of bright gorse separates field from heather upland. Continue to **RHYNIE**, sleeping gently round its village green, and **Lumsden**, another peaceful little community, disturbed only by its role as the venue for the Scottish Sculpture Workshop. Unexpected metal things lurk even in the roadside greenery. The A97 continues through the patchwork of fields on the edge of upland Aberdeenshire to reach the Mossat junction and starting point of this route.

# The Inner Moray Firth—the Moray 'Riviera'

*2–4 days/(at least) 135 miles (216km)/from the Grantown-on-Spey area*

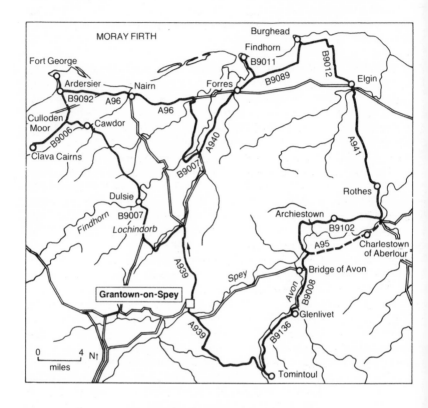

*This castle hath a pleasant seat; the air*
*Nimbly and sweetly recommends itself*
*Unto our gentle senses.*

from Shakespeare's *Macbeth*

In the heart of Scotland, the Grampian mountains at length give way to the sea along the Moray Firth. With the prevailing winds and rain from the south-west, this means the coastal strip of the old counties of Moray and Nairn—in what geographers call the 'rain-shadow' of the hills—is well-favoured with low rainfall and good records for sunshine. If the uplands to the south catch the rain, then the coastal strip has the climate for growing barley. Grain and water come together in the most obvious industry of the area: whisky distilling. This route covers the whisky country of Speyside, where wooded river valleys shelter strange complexes of warehousing, pagoda roofs, chimneys and the all-pervading warm reek of malt and steam. The area has a wealth of interest, making time planning difficult. You could actually drive this route in a day, but a castle, battle-site, distillery visit or a scenic stroll will play havoc with your schedule! Moray is one of Scotland's most rewarding touring-grounds. The route description starts from Grantown-on-Spey not because of any accommodation recommendation, though there is a wide choice, but because many visitors will reach the area via the main A9 which passes west of the town.

**GRANTOWN-ON-SPEY** is an example of a planned Highland town, well laid-out and stoutly built of granite amongst the tall Scots pines. Take A939 north, noting the views back to the Cairngorms beyond the point where the abandoned railway crosses the road on a bridge by Castle Grant's gates. Road and track-bed lead on to the wastes of Dava Moor. The track-bed was once the Highland Railway's main line to Inverness, before the direct route via Carrbridge and Slochd summit was built.

The Dava Moor section might be Act I, Scene I in *Macbeth*: 'A desert heath'—come to life. It is even near both Forres and Cawdor Castle. However, instead of three witches, look for a roadsign, left for **Lochindorb**. This soon winds on to a loch below the wide moorland sky and a grim ruin on an island. In 1371, the 13C fortress of **Lochindorb Castle**, once occupied by Edward of England, became the fortress of the notorious Wolf of Badenoch, Alexander Stewart, Earl of Buchan. This hot-tempered ruffian, close to the line of the Stewart monarchy, controlled the Highlands by terrorism and destruction.

Continue west to join B9007, right. If driving this way in springtime, watch for blue or mountain hares, quite as mad as their Lowland cousins and whose courtship rituals seem to preclude good road-sense. As the first of the upland pastures begin to confront the unimproved moor, look for a sign to **Dulsie Bridge**. This takes you left on to the former military road to Fort George (see below). Stands of birches begin to improve the scenery as you approach the River Findhorn. Look for a parking place on your left after Dulsie Lodge. Go through a kissing gate then walk a few yards to a viewpoint to Dulsie Bridge. Across the River Findhorn here went the military road, built in the 1750s and running to the new military base at Fort George. An information panel gives extra detail.

Follow the signs for Cawdor. Beyond the forestry and the thickets of birches and juniper, outstanding views open out north over the inner Moray Firth, a delightful and frequently repeated feature of much of this drive. Try to spot Fort George, to be visited later on its promontory to the north-west. By following Cawdor signs you drop off the timber-clad tableland to a softer and well-cultivated coastal strip to arrive at **Cawdor Castle**. This attractive, turreted and mellow edifice—the central tower dates from the 14C—has been home to the Campbells, Thanes (or Earls) of Cawdor, for 600 years. There is plenty of interest inside and out, from a mahogany wig-stand to the iron yett rescued from Lochindorb. (Lord Cawdor's Room Notes are a treat in themselves.) Diversion is also assured in the gardens and nature trails.

From the village of Cawdor, Culloden Moor is signed by way of B9090, then left at Clephanton on B9091 and left at Croy on B9006.

The battlefield of **Culloden**, the last major encounter fought on British soil, is in the care of the NTS. On a sleety spring day in 1746, Prince Charles Edward Stuart, badly advised, brought his 5,000 men to face the 9,000 regular soldiers of the Hanoverian army under the command of the Prince's distant cousin, General Cumberland. The business was soon over. Maimed by superior firepower, the Highland charge was ragged when it finally rolled and, for once, was easily resisted. After the battle, Cumberland gained the title 'Butcher' and the British army committed what have been described as the worst atrocities in its history on the local civilian population, Jacobite and Hanoverian alike. The excellent audio/visual presentation sets the battle in a historic perspective. This was no Scots versus English affair, but a battle in a civil war with political loyalties splitting families, irrespective of nationality. Lowland Scots regiments were at Cumberland's command and the Campbell militia also took the government side. Tour buses disgorge their creased-cardigan, stiff-limbed contents, the tills in the book- and gift-shop ring out and the teacups make a jolly rattle—but for all that, you may still find Culloden one of the most poignant places in all of Scotland.

Go south-east from the battlesite on a minor road, then turn left—do not go under the railway viaduct—and you will find an altogether more ancient site. The **Clava Cairns**, a great ring cairn and two passage graves all in a line in a wooded enclosure, date from the late Bronze Age.

*Fort George*

Retrace your route to Culloden, then east on B9006 to Croy and on north to cross—with care at a staggered junction—the main A96. B9006 leads to Ardersier and **Fort George**, which was the London government's answer to the problem of the rebellious Highlands. Part of a programme of disarming and proscription, it helped ensure that the Highland way of life was destroyed for ever. (A chief's lifestyle included the ability to call on a loyal private army, i.e. his clan. This fact seemed to make southern governments nervous!)

Fort George is one of the most complete military fortifications to be found anywhere in Europe. Work began on it in 1748 and took 21 years to complete. You can take in its visitor centre and the tableaux of military life, and stroll along the wall-tops, admiring sea-views from its parapets. Inside and below you is a complete military town, still garrisoned to this day. The **Regimental Museum of the Queen's Own Highlanders** is among other buildings to be visited within. While admiring the patterns of light and shadows on the walls as the angles change, it is easy to forget that the whole complex was a deadly exercise in the art of military defence, though it never fired a shot in anger.

Just south of Ardersier, go left on B9092 to rejoin the A96 to reach **NAIRN**. This community was once made up of twin settlements of fisherfolk by the river mouth and small farmers above. Then the Highland Railway pushed through its main line and the Victorians saw the potential of the sandy links and bracing climate for resort development. Today the harbour has only pleasure craft, while the story of the fishery is told in the friendly and informally informative **Fishertown Museum**. Plenty of holidaymakers still enjoy Nairn's beaches and golf courses. Just west of the A96 roundabout you will find **Nairn Antiques**, a signal that antiques browsers will find much to delay them from Nairn eastwards.

Take the main A96 east, across the prosperous rolling farmlands, passing **Auldearn** with a hilltop panorama board beside its doocot (dovecote) explaining the 1645 battle here when Montrose, taking the king's side, defeated the Covenanters. Shortly after, look for **Brodie Country Fare**, a quality all-day meal-stop which may also agreeably damage your holiday budget if you stray into its wide-ranging gifts and clothes section. A crossroads just beyond gives a further option: **Brodie Castle** is signed left. This NTS property is a 16C Z-plan structure with later extensions. It has a major painting collection as well as furniture and porcelain.

However, your route goes right, signed **Darnaway Farm Visitor Centre**. This farm complex on the edge of the wide woodlands of the Moray Estates gives an insight into the work of estate and farm management. Then follow unclassified roads through the forest by going right at the junction—signed Darnaway—beyond the farm, then left at the sign Whitemire, Redstone, Conicavel. The woods include stretches of tall beeches. Look for Darnaway Castle on the left, then follow this meandering back road until it reaches the rocky River Findhorn. Turn left across the bridge (good picnic spot) and climb out of the river valley to go left again by the Relugas Farm sign on B9007.

Look for a substantial pull-off on your right, close to the river which is through the tall trees, below you on the left. This attractive spot is **Randolph's Leap**. Here the force of the Findhorn is hemmed in by grey and water-polished pink-veined rocks. It is a sublimely beautiful spot, though if you visit with children, they, like the waters, should be closely confined. The name Randolph recalls Thomas Randolph, Earl of Moray. He was chasing Alastair Cumming who had raided Darnaway Castle. Randolph got the name but Cumming did the leaping: a not over-difficult feat if the choice is between a ten-foot downward jump over water or being skewered on a 14C broad-sword.

B9007 joins A940 for Forres. On the way it passes the **Dallas Dhu Distillery**. This is not a working distillery but a preserved monument to the industry, in the care of Historic Scotland. You may prefer its interpretative facilities to a visit to a real one which smells more, though not unpleasantly. Remember that this route eventually leads into Speyside, wall-to-wall with whisky-making.

**FORRES** wins 'Britain in Bloom' competitions with regularity and as well as a handsome town house and a choice of shopping has a local history museum. At the east end of the town, off the main A96, look for a sign to **Sueno's Stone**. This worn sandstone slab of 9C war-reporting has an extraordinary presence, helped by its height of about 20ft (6m). It is thought to record a victory by the locals over Norse settlers from Orkney. If the day is clear, then a digression to the **Califer Viewpoint** is recommended. Unfortunately not easy to find from Forres itself, proceed along the A96 east to find a signpost taking you right. Further signs lead in a circle to a high viewpoint on a broad shoulder of woods and farmlands with breathtaking views across the well-favoured 'Laich' (low coastal grounds) of Moray. Return to Forres, well in sight, by following the back roads directly downhill.

Take the coastal route from Forres by way of B9011 to **FINDHORN**, formerly accidentally famous for the giant vegetables which the spiritual community grew there. With an enclosed bay and long sandy beaches, it is also a popular water sports centre. B9089 at nearby Kinloss goes east to **BURGHEAD**. The regular arrangement of streets tells the visitor that this was yet another of Scotland's many planned settlements. Laid out 1805–9, the sleepy little town all but obliterated what historians think was Scotland's finest Pictish fort. A Pictish well can be visited and a few animal carvings survive, scattered in Scottish museums. Take B9012 to Elgin, across the once-marshy raised beach flats that protected both Pictish fort and the later alien culture of the Norman motte and bailey on which stands the gaunt stonework of 12/13C **Duffus Castle**, seen across the fields to your left.

**ELGIN**, the administrative centre of Moray, is a substantial and quite handsome town. Old-established, its original medieval street layout is preserved with a wide former market place and little lanes running off at right-angles. Its original parish church was replaced in 1825–8 by an impressive, or perhaps overbearing, 'Greek Revival' place of worship, complete with portico at one end and tower at the other. Traffic squeezes round both sides and past the Muckle Cross, a replica of the original mercat cross. A few shops with arcaded fronts also survive, particularly near the tourist information centre at the eastern end of the main street, and there are many other architectural details around the town as a reminder of its antiquity, including **Old Mills**, a preserved water mill with ancient origins. Dr Johnson, on his Scottish tour, passed through Elgin and was not over-enamoured with the cuisine. However, today's traveller should find a much better choice. For a quick and easy pub lunch for instance, try **Clouseau's**, up a 'close' off the High Street (towards the east end).

**Elgin Cathedral**, north of the main street, is a sad shell of what was perhaps the most beautiful medieval cathedral in Scotland. Founded in

1224, it was severely damaged by the Wolf of Badenoch (see Lochindorb Castle, p. 125), who burned it along with the town because he had been excommunicated by the local bishop. Though rebuilt, it later went the way of many pre-Reformation Scottish religious buildings, gradually pillaged and wantonly destroyed in the centuries thereafter.

On the theme of religious places, **Pluscarden Abbey**, south-west of the town and signed from the A96, represents a more optimistic note. Founded in 1230, it naturally underwent all the vicissitudes of Scottish history, including the attentions of the Wolf of Badenoch. Though empty and ruinous within a few decades of the Reformation, it was settled again by monks from Prinknash near Gloucester in 1948 and restored thereafter. It now houses an active religious community.

If you visit Pluscarden, return to Elgin to take A941 south through the Glen of Rothes, passing the nature trails and woodlands of **Millbuies**— good picnic sites. As you approach **ROTHES** and the River Spey, you are entering whisky country. For confirmation, open the car windows and sniff the air as you pass through this peacefully undistinguished little town, wrapped in a malty, warm reek—not at all unpleasant. This all-pervading atmosphere might come from the **Glen Grant Distillery**, which offers tours, samples and a reception centre.

It must be noted that many of the distilleries around Speyside welcome visitors and several have well-developed visitor facilities. Though some offer tours only by appointment, others offer sophisticated presentations and, taken altogether, there is a very wide choice. Continue by the Spey to Craigellachie, noting Thomas Telford's fine suspension bridge, which the main road now bypasses. Cross the river for **ABERLOUR** (marked as Charlestown of Aberlour on maps), a short way right and upstream on the A95. Here you can visit the **Village Store**, no ordinary shop but a slightly sad time-capsule in which stock from decades ago—mainly hardware and clothing—was locked away when the business was closed. New owners decided to put the wares on display, original packaging in original shop-fittings, and the result is a little eerie. Nearby is the **Old Pantry** (03405 617), which serves anything from a scone and jam to a four-course dinner in relaxing and informal surroundings. (Best to book in the evenings.)

You can continue on the A95 to Marypark (see below), or retrace your route a little way back to Craigellachie and over the Spey to take B9102, left, signed Archiestown. This gives good views of Ben Rinnes, southwards and left, the guardian hill of the Spey's middle reaches. Nearer at hand the road crosses wooded uplands and pasture to pass the **Ladycroft Agricultural Museum**, recalling the days of horse-drawn farm implements. The premises stand on a rise to your right. The road returns to the Spey—cross it on B9138 for Marypark and turn right on A95, by which time you will be well-attuned to spotting distillery signs. Glen Grant, Cardhu, Tamdhu, Glenfarclas and many more make a list with just as much distinction as the vineyards of the Rhône Valley.

Speyside offers continually improving scenic delights, with

birch-sheltered farmlands by the river edged with woods and plantations running well up the flanks of rounded heathery hills. Still some distance from the Cairngorms, they are not yet intimidatingly bare. The distilleries blend reasonably well into the landscape and provide local employment, so that the area is not quite dominated by the incomer or holiday-cottage economy. To enjoy further harmonious 'riverscapes', take B9008 left at Bridge of Avon, signed for Tomintoul. This follows the Spey tributary of the River Avon, which (as in Bridge of Avon or Ben Avon) must be pronounced 'Aan' with a long 'a'.

By following signs to the Glenlivet Distillery, you turn right on to B9136, crossing the River Livet, and within moments go left on an unclassified road at the sign for **Minmore House** (08073 378). This was the former home of George Smith, the founder of the original distillery. Now it is a country house hotel of high quality. Its original owner might not have approved of the range of malt whisky competitors on the shelves of its discreetly furnished, dark-panelled bar. However, the choice gives guests the opportunity of musing over exactly why a single malt is interesting enough before dining, but attains the status of liquid philosophy after dinner. At Minmore, it could, of course, be the high quality of the cuisine itself.

Late in the evening, if you stay here, step out for a moment into the pure upland air. Along the road, beyond the bleating sheep, the **Glenlivet Distillery** looks a little extra-terrestrial—gleaming tanks and orange glow with a lick of steam. (You do not have to have been drinking the product to think this.) Visit it by day and you will find guided tours, exhibits of whisky-making artefacts, a video presentation, reception centre, samples and a gift and coffee shop. Further up the road, which rejoins B9008, you will find the **Tamnavulin Distillery** (also with a visitor centre)—but then, further up any glen hereabouts, you will find another distillery!

Two roads lead from Glenlivet to Tomintoul and the more attractive is reached by returning to the river at the B9136/B9008 junction, taking B9136 upstream. All around, the birch trees crowd thickly. In spring the silvered branches are half hidden by a haze of swelling buds of a curious plum or aubergine tint when seen in mass. The tweedy colours of tree and hill hereabouts are further enhanced by glimpses of the river. Strath Avon certainly offers high-grade scenery.

At the junction with the A939, your loop is completed by going right for Grantown-on-Spey. However, **TOMINTOUL** is a little way down the road on the left. This planned village is the highest in the Highlands (though not in Scotland, see p. 34). It sits ringed by hills—look for distant Ben Avon, on your right, southwards, whose long slopes, broken by distinctive tors, hold snow until late in the year. Tomintoul also has a local museum. It also is the place, along with Cockbridge, which has a certain notoriety as it seems to be mentioned most often on Radio Scotland when reports on routes closed by snow are broadcast. In fact, the A939 Tomintoul-Cockbridge road is an interesting excursion to link with the 'Grampian castles' route on p. 114. It goes via the Lecht, an optimistic ski development on not over-high moorland.

Going the other way on A939, having retraced your route from Tomintoul, you travel via Bridge of Brown over high moorland domes, marbled like a chocolate sponge, and leading soon to a superb open view of Speyside, a dark green swathe to the north-west. Follow the road down to its junction with A95, just south of Grantown-on-Spey.

# Shetland—the Ultimate Islands

*3 days (not including journey to Scotland)/(at least) 140 miles (224km)/from Lerwick*

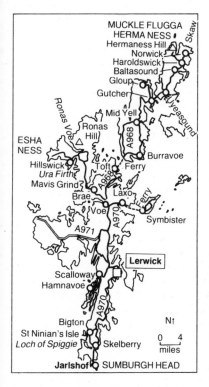

*Da girse aye grows far greener here*
*Dan ony idder wye*
*An da sun aye sheens far brichter*
*Oot o da simmer sky.*
From the Shetland dialect poems
of Rhoda Bulter

You cannot be neutral about Shetland. You will either love it for its constant involvement with the sea, or hate it—intimidated by empty northerly skies and austere landscapes. A 900-mile (1,440km) coastline is Shetland's chief focus of interest—inevitably, as nowhere is more than 3 miles (5km) from the sea. Apart from Lerwick, its chief town, and perhaps also Scalloway, settlements are small and scattered, and accommodation and restaurant choices limited in places. Trees are stunted or missing entirely. However, try to see these factors as positive attractions which all add to the unique and haunting atmosphere of the islands.

In fact, Shetland is one of the most beautiful places in Britain, especially if you are a great skua, puffin, gannet, whimbrel, arctic tern, or any one of dozens of other species which force themselves upon your attention. Shetland has nothing to do with the Gaelic experience of the Hebrides and little to do with the Scottish mainland. Visit Shetland and you travel overseas to another country with strong Scandinavian links. Happily, the folk are very friendly. Ask directions and you may well be invited in for a cup of tea. It certainly happened to me on Yell.

In advance of the trip you should work out the relative costs of taking your own car by sea or hiring when you arrive. Full information from

**P&O Ferries**, Scottish Services, 5 Jamieson's Quay, Aberdeen (0224 572615). Car hire in Shetland can be safely recommended from **Star Rent-A-Car**, 22 Commercial Road, Lerwick (0595 2075). The **Shetland Tourist Organisation**, Information Centre, Lerwick (0595 3434) can also advise on special holiday packages. Finally, you can fly direct from Aberdeen. Remember that the islands are perhaps bigger than you think. It is, for example, 52 miles (83km) from Lerwick to Baltasound in the north of Unst, a journey which involves two inter-island ferries (very cheap but you are advised to *book in advance* with either the Shetland Tourist Organisation or by telephoning 0957 82259/82268 in office hours).

By sea, you reach Shetland after a 14-hour overnight voyage from **Aberdeen**—sleeping accommodation is recommended. The P&O ferry arrives at **LERWICK**. This is the largest town, founded in the 17C after the Dutch used the bay as a fishing base and a trading post was set up. The port is sheltered by the island of Bressay. Lerwick has narrow flagged streets behind a sprawling workaday harbourfront, a good shopping choice (this is no frontier outpost—you *can* buy colour slide film!), some surviving 18C buildings complete with 'lodberries' (private piers) and the well-preserved bulwarks of **Fort Charlotte**, a 17C Cromwellian fort. It also has a good local **museum** and the **Bod of Gremista**, a severe-looking restored 18C merchant's house, unhappily a little isolated in the midst of marine yards on the shore. Outside the town, overlooked by modern housing—a reminder of the islands' partly oil-based prosperity—is **Clickhimin Broch**, a mysterious Pictish monument with a complicated series of habitation. Brochs are northern fortified round towers whose purpose is not clear, some writers describing them as a response to a sea-borne threat, others as simply a defensive development in the war-like world which prevailed (very approximately) from 500BC to AD500. Most brochs are now greatly ruined.

Take A970 south from Lerwick, passing Clickhimin and enjoying views opening up of the cliffs at the south end of the island of Bressay. This is a wide and easy road which separates green fields running down to a rocky shore on your left, from bare moors on your right. Before reaching Sandwick, look left for the little island of **Mousa**, on which stands the best-preserved example of a broch anywhere in Scotland. You can see the **Mousa Broch** like a distant upturned flower-pot by the shore. Boat trips go from Sandwick to visit it. Continuing south, look for a sign, left on to a minor road, to the **Shetland Croft Museum**, an excellent starting point for an appreciation of the former way of life of the rural Shetlander. As well as a range of artefacts in this traditionally constructed dwelling, with byre and corn-drying kiln attached, there is much to be learned from the custodians. A short walk across the fields from the croft takes you to the community's former watermill. All the aspects of milling—water source, wheel blades and grinding stone—are miniaturised. The simple horizontal wheel is no more than a water-powered quern or hand-mill.

Continue on the minor road which loops back to rejoin A970. (Nearby, the local grocery store offers a good cup of tea.) Continue towards **Sumburgh Head**, past the airport, busy with helicopters ferrying oil-workers. (Little more than 20 years ago, the sheep had to be chased off the landing strip before a plane arrived. Now there is a grand terminal building, helicopter servicing and all the paraphernalia of a busy airport.)

Look for the sign to **Jarlshof** by the airport. This fascinating, complex seashore site was revealed after a storm in 1905. Though the most obvious survivor is the 17C laird's house, there is evidence of a medieval farmstead, extensive remains of Norse buildings, as well as much earlier wheelhouses and prehistoric earthhouses, suggesting continuous occupation for thousands of years.

Afterwards, continue on to a single-track road which leads to the hump of Sumburgh Head. Park where the road ends, before it goes into the lighthouse ground. If you look over the wall on the right, beside the telegraph pole and the first hairpin beyond the lighthouse wall, you should see puffins. If, as I did, you look over the cliff to the left and see an otter in the surf below (definitely not a seal—it had a tail) then that is a bonus!

Afterwards, retrace your route as far as Skelberry, going left on B9122, signed for Bigton, then left again for the RSPB reserve at **Loch of Spiggie**. This is perhaps the place to make your acquaintance with another Shetland speciality—the bonxie. This is the local name for the great skua, a swaggering and fearless air-pirate like a bulky brown gull. There are usually a few loitering on the loch. Note that this low-lying stretch of water was once a sea-inlet and is only yards from a beautiful beach—one of many in Shetland. Return to B9122 and continue north. There are other white-sand beaches on the way, as well as outstanding views of the island of **Foula**. This pleasant road continues to the spectacle of **St Ninian's Isle**, moored to Mainland by a dazzling cream 'tombolo', a back-to-back beach or sand-spit, the finest example of its kind in the UK. Excavations of a ruined medieval kirk in the 1950s revealed the St Ninian's Treasure, 28 silver objects buried for safekeeping beneath the nave.

Afterwards, return to the main road and Lerwick. The **Kvelsdro House Hotel** (0595 2195), near the harbour, offers friendly service and well-cooked bar meals at lunchtimes—try the breaded haddock.

Set out from Lerwick again, taking A970 northwards to explore the western coastline. Follow signs for **SCALLOWAY**, the old 'capital', stopping at a main road viewpoint (with panorama board) which overlooks its harbour and castle. **Scalloway Castle** was built in 1600 by an unwilling local labour force for the Earl Patrick (to whom history has given a cruel reputation). He was executed in 1615 and afterwards the castle fell into disrepair. The key-keeper of this draughtily impressive monument lives round the corner. Next door is the **Shetland Woollen Manufacturing Company** which sells a good range of traditional knitwear.

A970 loses itself in the narrow side streets of the little community beyond. Retrace your route as far as B9074, right, signed Trondra. The islands of East and West Burra and Trondra are joined by bridges and are prosperous-looking places by the sea. The road to Hamnavoe gives outstanding views of an interlacing of islands to the north, while the road at West Burra ends at **Papil**. There is a rough car park beyond which is a little gate. If you go through it and walk across the fenced path through a field, you find another of Shetland's beautiful beaches. This one gives views to Foula and is popular with Lerwick folk on sunny Sunday afternoons—which Shetland *does* have.

Return to your Lerwick base. Accommodation in Lerwick is quite wide-ranging, some of it catering for oil executives and successful local skippers looking for a good night out. For example, the modern and disconcertingly multi-levelled **Shetland Hotel** (0595 5515) offers very high standards of accommodation and is ideally placed only moments from the ferry terminal.

From Lerwick, you must make your choice of the smaller islands, as well as explore further the main island, which is usually referred to as Mainland. Take A970 north and look for the turn-off, for West Mainland, the A971. (It is at the top of a hill.) Note how the brown landscapes turn green with a band of limestone in the valley. Two attractions by the road are **Hjaltasteyn**, handcrafted jewellery and gemstones, on the left overlooking the narrowing Weisdale Voe, and **Shetland Silvercraft** on the right shortly afterwards. (They also have a shop in Lerwick.)

Take B9075 at the head of the voe (a narrow sea-inlet) which leads into the green valley of **Kergord**. This is famed for its trees, which would pass unremarked on the Scottish mainland. Hereabouts the sycamores, horse chestnuts and conifers huddled together have great novelty value. Continue on B9075 to rejoin A970, turning left. This leads via dark moorlands to another burst of bright emerald at **Voe**, another Scandinavian-flavoured settlement at the head of a long inlet or firth. (There is another Shetland knitwear company here.)

Drive on to **Brae**, a long scatter near the head of Sullom Voe, which is a name associated with the North Sea oil developments. These have changed the face of many small places—now with their drifts of new housing and gleaming community centres. The main road goes left and west, with a minor road to Muckle Roe going left again. Just off this road is the **Busta House Hotel** (080622 506), a historic house built by the local lairds and dating in part from the 16C, with later building phases. It is sheltered by trees and overlooks Busta Voe. Though not inexpensive, it certainly offers a sophisticated cuisine and a warm and pleasing ambience. The staff are also friendly and helpful.

Beyond, northwards, the main road goes over **Mavis Grind**. This is where two inlets, one the North Sea, the other the Atlantic—loosely speaking—come within stone-throwing distance of each other, if you have an extremely strong arm. After that, the route heads into loch-dappled moors—look for red-throated divers, which breed by lonely inland waters. There are also distant views of the Sullom Voe oil terminal, glowering and flaring across the dark hills. Follow A970 left for

**HILLSWICK**. Here in a scattering of houses, an old pub and a church, is the **St Magnus Bay Hotel** (080623 372), whose bar-lunch whole plaice cooked on the bone hangs over the edge of the plate and is fresh enough to wink at the customer. The hotel is in authentic Scandinavian pinewood-panelled style.

The north-west shoulder of Mainland is noted for its cliff scenery. Retrace your route a little way to go left at B9078, which goes over open moors, with plenty of bird life, and gives views southwards of extraordinary fangs and sandstone cliff-columns. There is also a cluster of stacks, well away from the shore, which may remind you of a Viking galley under sail. Park by the lighthouse at **Esha Ness** and walk northwards over tightly cropped turf—easy walking—for a flavour of the extraordinary cliffs, where storms, rain and frost have made great shattered quarries and deep inlets.

On your return from Esha Ness, rejoin A970 above Hillswick, going left, then go left again along a minor road from the head of Ura Firth. This gives good views of the bare red flanks of **Ronas Hill**, the highest hill in Shetland, though only 1,486ft (460m), and a Site of Special Scientific Interest for its plantlife—hereabouts, arctic-alpine flora grows at low levels. Go right along Ronas Voe/Orr Wick to rejoin A970. Turn right, south, and drive back through Brae, to Voe.

To the south of Voe, B9071 goes east (left) to Laxo, the ferry port for the island of **Whalsay**. (Tel. 08066 259 to book ferry.) This is a very interesting island as it is one of the most prosperous, thanks mainly to the highly-profitable, modern and sophisticated fishing vessels whose crews live there. **Lingaveg Guest House** (08066 489), a former manse, is a very welcoming and relaxed establishment and makes a good base for exploring the island. There are a few prehistoric sites, a good selection of birdlife on the moors and, overlooking the harbour at Symbister, the **Bremen Bod**. This 17C trading booth (cf bod) has been restored as a visitor centre. It depicts the past trading life of the harbour here which, like many other Shetland harbours on this great sea crossroads, was important in the days of the Hanseatic League. (This was a confederation of trading ports around the North Sea. At its height merchants from many Baltic ports traded in Shetland during the summer, hence the surviving 'bods.' The Hanseatic trade ended in the early 18C.)

Having covered the Mainland area from Sumburgh in the south to Esha Ness in the north-west and also diverted to Whalsay, if time permits, an excursion to the northern island group is very rewarding. The two vehicle-ferries operating Mainland–Yell and Yell–Unst are not large. However, they run frequently and are heavily subsidised. You might not always need to, but it will make the trip more relaxed if you book your vehicle across using the telephone number given above.

Take A970 north to the junction with A968 just north of Voe. Follow this road north again to **Toft**, the ferry-pier for **Ulsta** on the island of **Yell**. Two-thirds of this island is blanket-bog. The other portion is very interesting. Find this out for yourself by taking B9081 east to **BURRA-VOE**. Follow the road towards the shore to visit the **Old Haa of Burra-voe**. Haa is Scots for hall and this building, the oldest on Yell, is now a museum with changing exhibitions depicting the life of the community. The local ladies staffing the little café within are also a useful source of information. On your way north, up the B9081, for instance, they will tell you where to look out for the **White Wife**. A copy of her stands outside the Old Haa, while the much-restored original looks over Otters Wick: she is the figurehead of a German sail-training ship, the *Bohus*, wrecked there in 1924. A white figure leaning into the shore-winds, look for her from the main road near Queyon.

B9081 rejoins the main road at Mid Yell, from where you proceed north to Gutcher and the next ferry. If time permits here, it is worth going both ways at the Gutcher crossroads—right to Easter House, for views towards Burra Ness and if you have binoculars, a ruined broch on the headland: left, for a very pleasant drive by green fields and yellow marsh-marigolds to the road-end at Gloup. You may have noticed a sign at the Gutcher crossroads to the **Gloup Fishermen's Memorial**. At Gloup there is no sign of it, as it is tucked behind a croft on a grassy shoulder overlooking Gloup Voe. (Just ask one of the friendly locals for more details.) The memorial recalls an 1881 fishing disaster when ten local six-oared fishing boats, 'sixerenes', were lost with all hands.

Return to Gutcher to take the ferry to Belmont on the island of **Unst**. The most northerly inhabited island in Scotland is quite a cheery place. There is a substantial military presence, though the listening posts and tracking stations peering into the North Atlantic do not particularly intrude. Take A968 as far as B9084, right for Uyeasound and the sign-posted **Muness Castle**, the most northerly in Scotland. (You can have

much amusement spotting 'most northerly' objects in Unst.) The castle was built in 1598 by Laurence Bruce and was burnt, perhaps by a French privateer force, within a century. There are also good views across to the cliffs of the island of **Fetlar**, famous in recent years for its snowy owls, on the very southern edge of their range.

Returning to the main road, go right and then left for Westing (a cul-de-sac road). The ruined medieval **Kirk of Lund** lies on the south shore of Lunna Wick, while, branching right for Westing, the **Irvings** at **Barns, Newgord** (095785 249) offer a comfortable,

*Snowy owl*

relaxed and very informal dinner, bed and breakfast, which includes one of the best sunset views from anyone's kitchen sink anywhere.

A968 continues northwards across bare lands to **BALTASOUND**, a small settlement, boosted by RAF personnel, where the blue waters of Balta Sound spill into a shallow green bowl. The northern shore climbs gently to the dome of the **Keen of Hamar**, another nature reserve where normally high-level plant communities and weathered rock are found only a little above sea level.

However, the main interest will be to reach the most northerly point— either by car or on foot. To reach the car's most northerly point, at **Haroldswick** (most northerly **post-office**, most northerly **Heritage Centre**) go right for B9087 for **Norwick** (second-most northerly attractive sandy beach) and **Skaw** (most northerly house) and the end of the road. Retrace your route to Haroldswick, to take B9086 going right and westwards, then round the head of Burra Firth to the end of the road on the west side of the inlet. Press on 100 yards beyond the turning area to find a large car park. Depending on the time of day, you may find it filled with earnest soberly dressed folk bearing huge telescopes. They are birdwatchers, and like you, are going to **Herma Ness**, from where there are views to **Muckle Flugga**, the offshore stack, lighthouse-topped, at the very end of Scotland.

Wear sensible shoes and climb the 600ft (186m) Hermaness Hill—by which time you are further north than Skaw—across a rough moor patterned like a camouflage jacket and patrolled by aggressive great skuas (bonxies) determined to keep you out of their breeding territories. They dive-bomb intruders, a phenomenon well-known to birdwatchers and sheep but very unnerving for the casual visitor. Raising your hand suddenly above your head disconcerts a swooping bonxie and makes it swerve to one side. Please keep to the marked path—this is a National Nature Reserve.

From the top of Hermaness Hill the rough grounds fall away on all sides. Muckle Flugga appears northwards as the last of a link of tilting triangles drenched with guano and gannets. Taking great care on the hill's lower stretch, follow a path down left and westwards which leads to steepening, tightly cropped turf. Enjoy the birdlife—try not to disturb the friendly puffins on their cliff-edge nesting burrows and take great care on the grass that teeters and falls suddenly away to the sea. This is the top of Scotland, the ultimate northland, only 300 miles (480km) from the Arctic Circle. It is a place of wild grandeur which belongs to the gannets and the other wild seabirds.

Retrace your path over the hilltop, back to the car, and then back to Lerwick via two ferries—and eventually the softer landscapes of the Scottish mainland.

# A HISTORICAL NOTE

**AD1057—Scotland united** Stone circles and hill-forts, even the faint outline of Roman remains (see p. 000), are a reminder that Scotland had a long history well before King Malcom III defeated a Pictish chief in Moray, a certain Macbeth (later to inspire Shakespeare), in 1059. With this victory he brought together a number of warring kingdoms whose collective boundaries were much as they stand today.

**11th–13th centuries—first links with England** The king became known as Canmore—Great Head. He had a penchant for laying waste Northumbria, proving that conflict along the Border took place from very early times. He married Princess Margaret, of Alfred of England's royal line, thereby introducing the blood links with England which were to be the bane of Scotland ever after. This pattern was repeated more than once—for example their youngest son, King David also married into the, by then Anglo-Norman, court of England. Norman influence spread north thereafter, with the old Celtic ways retreating westwards. The idea of feudalism took root, burghs with trading rights were founded, the churches reorganised and abbeys built.

**Towards Bannockburn (1314)** The civilising Norman influence and the comparative peace ended in 1286 with the death of Alexander III. King Edward I of England, aware of the historical blood-links between the two courts, acted to claim Scotland as his vassal. By the end of the 13C a Scottish puppet-king had knelt in homage before the English throne. Out of the invasions and bloodshed arose the first Scottish freedom-fighter, William Wallace, only to be claimed by treachery and obscenely put to death. Goaded further into resistance by the English Plantagenets, the Scots united under Robert the Bruce, who led the nation to victory on a hot and dusty June day in 1314. The Battle of Bannockburn is still remembered by nationalist rallies each year, though it was but one triumph in a long history of defeats. Scots mark the event as the beginning of the nation's period of independence—though England refused to acknowledge it at the time.

**The Stewart monarchs** Robert the Bruce's daughter married Walter the High Steward of Scotland and thus ushered in the Stewart dynasty, whose speciality was dying inconveniently while their offspring were too young to rule. This sparked off successive power struggles between Scotland's noble families and encouraged the Highland chiefs to act as independent rulers within their own fastnesses. Notable misfortunes included the defeat of the Scots under King James IV at Flodden in 1513, when they were slaughtered for siding with the French. This lesson was not learned by King James V, who insisted on taking a French wife— twice—thereby feeling obliged to side with France again against King Henry VIII of England. This resulted in yet another defeat for the Scots— Solway Moss 1542. Worse, Henry VIII then decided it was a good idea to marry off his infant son to the equally infant Mary Queen of Scots, thereby uniting the two kingdoms. Even Henry's subtle gambit of burning four Border abbeys and much of Edinburgh failed to make the Scots see his point of view. The young Mary—the best known and most romantic of the Stewarts (whose name was changed to the French spelling, Stuart)—was taken to France in 1548 for safety. As a Catholic and already-widowed queen, she returned in 1561 to a faction-ridden Scotland in the throes of the Reformation. Her brief reign in that country (1561–8) ended in exile and her execution in England, though not before many trips around Scotland, for which several stately homes and later guide-book writers were extremely grateful. Her son, who became King James VI, later inherited the English throne on the death of his mother's cousin, Queen Elizabeth of England—hence the Union of the Crowns in 1603.

**Towards the United Kingdom** James VI (I of England) took his court to England in 1603 and from his southern base continued to be an opponent of the new religious thinking in Scotland. His son, Charles I, went too far in his opposition to religious reforms, precipitating the Scots into signing a declaration of their opposition: the National Covenant (supported by the Covenanters). Scotland's 17C history is particularly complex and in many ways inseparable from England's. Scottish forces played a part in the English Civil Wars of 1642–51. Prominent historical figures of the age included David Leslie, commanding the Covenanters against the king, and James Graham, Marquis of Montrose, who sided with the king and led brilliant military campaigns. However, many Scots who supported the National Covenant still believed the king had his role in church and state, and thus, after the execution of Charles I in 1649, the Scots declared his son king, forcing the English Parliamentarian leader Oliver Cromwell to invade. English troops again garrisoned Scotland. Eventually, after the Restoration in 1660, King Charles II bitterly opposed the Covenanting movement (particularly strong in the south-west.)

**The Jacobites and the union with England** King James VII (II of England) continued the encouragement of Catholicism, which many Highland clans supported. Even after his overthrow and a new order under King William, his supporters, the Jacobites (Latin Jacobus = James) stirred up the Highlands and beyond. The first conflict of the Jacobite campaigns took place in 1689—the Battle of Killiecrankie, though the Jacobite clans were unable to follow up their victory on the field. The clans continued to be seen as troublesome by Lowland authorities on both sides of the Border in an increasingly mercantile and commercial age and thus the unlucky Macdonalds were made an example of in the shameful episode in Glen Coe—see p. 71. Meanwhile, Scotland seemed at a disadvantage in matters of trade compared to her richer neighbour in the south.

One important factor in Scotland's story—and one often underemphasised—is the ill-fated Darien Scheme. The nation—particularly the nobility—sunk its wealth into a misguided effort at colonisation on the isthmus of Panama. Much to England's relief, Scotland's attempt at mercantile independence failed. Worse, the nation was greatly weakened financially with, in crude terms, its powerful families active in politics only too eager to 'sell out' to England, keen on a complete union. Scotland wanted stronger trading rights and hinted that if they were not granted then the people would choose their own monarch—a broad hint that they would entertain the exiled Stuart king, the Jacobite 'Pretender' waiting on the continent. At the same time, political union would give the country the trading links it required. In this complex political situation the Scots Parliament voted 110 to 67 in favour of a Union. Scotland as a separate nation ceased to exist. Several of Scotland's great families had their debts paid off, later prompting Robert Burns to write a still frequently heard song with the bitter refrain:

> We are bought and sold for English gold
> Such a Parcel of Rogues in a Nation.

**The last rebellions** Jacobitism was never a narrow Scottish movement: powerful Catholic European nations were waiting to lend it support. France was the main hope of the Scots Jacobites for decades. Also political opportunists at Westminster could exhort it as a kind of 'bogeyman' in much the same way as 'the threat from the east' is used to justify political stances today. Likewise it was a cause for other opportunists to rally round—such as the Earl of Mar, 'Bobbing John' of ballad fame, who initiated the indecisive rebellion of 1715. There were further near-misses (weather at sea never seemed to favour foreign powers' attempts at invasions of Britain) and minor episodes until the 'rash adventurer', Prince Charles Edward Stuart, set off for Scotland in 1745. He landed on Eriskay and was promptly told to go home. He said he had come home and thereby confirmed his romantic image. After gathering support he marched via Perth and Stirling to Edinburgh, defeated the government forces at nearby Prestonpans and crossed over the Border. He got as far as Derby, with King George in London packed and ready to jump aboard the Royal Yacht. Thereafter, the Prince's fortunes changed and were blown away at Culloden in the following year.

Close reading of contemporary accounts gives the impression that the ordinary folk of Scotland were a bit sceptical of this impetuous young man. Going about their business, perhaps as farmworkers learning new agricultural practices, masons helping to create beautiful neo-classical buildings or mill-workers adjusting to the hard routines of industry, they may even have considered it just a sideshow.

**The Highland Clearances** Charles's mad adventure brings the high drama of Scottish history to a close, except for the 19C Highland Clearances, when once again, the Highlands suffered under the greed of the landowners. This new breed of entrepreneur sought profit from turning clan lands into sheepwalks, needing little manpower. However, even without the accelerated depopulation brought about by these shameful evictions and forced transportation, voluntary emigration took place from the mid-18C onwards because of the breakdown of the clan system and other adverse economic factors affecting the Highlands.

**Modern Scotland** To this day, Scotland keeps its own identity—and still remembers old wounds. The Scottish National Party undergoes periodic resurgences of support and is certainly a force in Scottish politics. Without necessarily supporting that party's views, many native-born folk consider themselves Scots first, with their citizenship of the United Kingdom second. Look in the 'Nationality' column in any hotel or tourist attraction visitors' book to see this for yourself.

# A SHORT BIBLIOGRAPHY

Scottish bookshops often have a large section marked 'Scottish', separate from 'Travel'—as there is a wide selection of material with a Scottish theme. The books listed here are only examples of the wide range of background information readily available.

## Historical Background

**Scottish Kings**, *Gordon Donaldson* (Batsford). A readable and balanced account of the Scottish monarchy from the 11C to King James VI and the union with England.

**Robert the Bruce**, *Ronald McNair Scott* (Hutchinson). Thorough picture of the greatest of Scotland's patriots.

**The Making of the Scottish Countryside**, *M. Parry and T. Slater* (eds) (Croom Helm). Academic and methodical, traces the evolution of the landscape from early field systems to rural industries.

**A History of the Scottish People 1560–1830**, *T.C. Smout* (Fontana Press). Very informative, wide-ranging and useful. Vital background material.

**The Lion in the North**, *John Prebble* (Secker & Warburg). Vivid and idiosyncratic account of Scottish history on a grand scale.

**Mercat Cross and Tolbooth**, *Craig Mair* (John Donald). Vital reading for a proper understanding of Lowland Scotland and its burghs.

**Clans and Chiefs**, *Ian Grimble* (Blond & Briggs). A useful separation of fact and fiction.

**Scotland's Roman Remains**, *Lawrence Keppie* (John Donald). A fascinating account of the Roman efforts to subdue the wild northern tribes.

**The Jacobite Risings in Britain 1689–1746**, *Bruce Lenman* (Methuen). The important role of Scotland in the wider European context of Jacobitism. Fascinating and complex.

**History of Highland Dress**, *J. Telfer Dunbar* (Batsford). A very authoritative account which demolishes some tartan mythology. Invaluable for also pointing out that the modern kilt was invented by an Englishman.

## Regional Guides

**Aberdeen: An Illustrated Architectural Guide**, *W. Brogden* (RIAS Landmark Guides). Thorough and well researched, and only one of an excellent series (some written by the series editor C. McKean—e.g. **Stirling and the Trossachs**) which inject wit and pleasing historical detail into the descriptions of buildings.

**Discovering Galloway**, *Innes MacLeod* (John Donald). Galloway is a well-detailed and readable example in another very informative regional series covering most of Scotland.

**Portrait of the Clyde**, *Jack House* (Robert Hale). Part of a regional series, this guide is a reminder that there is much more to the Clyde than the Clydeside conurbation and its shipbuilding traditions. Also in the same series: **Portrait of the Moray Firth**, *Cuthbert Graham*. A particularly well-researched evocation of the coastal strip around the UK's largest east coast sea-opening.

**Edinburgh: The Story of a City**, *E.F. Catford* (Hutchinson). A very thorough and entertaining account of Scotland's capital city.

**The Scottish Highlands**, *W.H. Murray* (Scottish Mountaineering Trust). Thorough and informative guide by one of Scotland's finest mountain writers.

**Skye**, *Derek Cooper* (Routledge & Kegan Paul). Gazetteer, anthology and over-view by an enthusiast.

**Exploring Scotland's Heritage**, *Anna Ritchie* (series ed.) (HMSO). A wonderfully concise and well-illustrated series covering a broad spectrum from prehistoric sites to industrial heritage. Available in a series of eight.

## Aspects of Scotland, Including Language and Landscape

**Scots: The Mither Tongue**, *Billy Kay* (Mainstream Publishing). Thought-provoking (and, to the native Scot, unsettling) account of the social and political history of the Scots language.

**The Concise Scots Dictionary**, *Mairi Robinson* (ed.-in-chief) (Aberdeen University Press). This recently published reference book has helped renew interest in the Scots language.

**The Story of Scotland's Hills**, *Campbell Steven* (Robert Hale). Fascinating background material for car-borne or hill-walking visitors.

**Munro's Tables**, *J.C. Donaldson* (ed.) (Scottish Mountaineering Trust). All of Scotland's hills over 3,000ft (930m) in height classified and arranged by height and district.

**A Pattern of Landownership in Scotland**, *Robin Fraser Callander* (Haughend Publications). A revealing study of Scotland's curious and unique system of landownership.

**The West Highland Railway**, *John Thomas* (David & Charles). Entertaining account (even for non-train-buffs) of the construction of Scotland's most scenic line.

**The Ballad and the Plough**, *David Kerr Cameron* (Gollancz). An evocative account of life on Scotland's farmtouns in former days.

**Country Life in Rural Scotland: Our Rural Past**, *Alexander Fenton* (John Donald). A wide-ranging and very informative portrayal of the development of agriculture in Scotland.

**Scotch Whisky: Its Past and Present**, *David Daiches* (Fontana/Collins).

Perhaps the standard work on the history and development of one of Scotland's leading exports.

**Geology and Scenery in Scotland**, *J.B. Whittow* (Penguin). Probably the most useful book in this short bibliography for visitors seeking to understand the landscapes of Scotland.

**The Scottish Castle**, *Stewart Cruden* (Spurbooks). An authoritative account of its evolution.

**New Ways Through the Glens**, *A.R.B. Haldane* (David & Charles). A well-researched account of the opening-up of the Highlands and the role of the engineer Thomas Telford. Of particular interest to today's car-borne travellers.

# INDEX

# Index